Edmund Lee

Some Noble Sisters

Edmund Lee

Some Noble Sisters

ISBN/EAN: 9783337778194

Printed in Europe, USA, Canada, Australia, Japan

Cover: Foto ©Thomas Meinert / pixelio.de

More available books at **www.hansebooks.com**

SOME NOBLE SISTERS

BY

EDMUND LEE,

Author of "Dorothy Wordsworth."

"And were another childhood world my share,
I would be born a little sister there."

GEORGE ELIOT.

London:
JAMES CLARKE & CO., 13 & 14, FLEET STREET.
1892.

PREFACE.

THE object of the present slight work is to gather together, from various available sources, records of the lives of some of the world's notable Sisters. It does not pretend to be by any means exhaustive, but rather suggestive. The Editor hopes that, while it may be found to be interesting reading generally, to young women, for whom it is more especially designed, it may be stimulating and consoling. The absence of such a record hitherto can alone justify the appearance of this fragmentary and imperfect work. Such as it is, its preparation has necessitated no small amount of labour and research. If it should be the means of quickening some life, or of arousing some sleeping affection to a warmer zeal, or more active devotion, its object will be answered.

The sources from which information has been obtained are varied. It should be stated that, in regard to the sketch of Susanne Kossuth, the facts are chiefly taken from a little work published many years ago in Boston, U.S.A. As to Eugénie de Guérin, the authorities are "Eugénie de Guérin:

Journal and Fragments"; "Lettres d'Eugénie de Guérin"; and "Maurice de Guérin : Journal, Lettres, et Poemes," all published by Mons. Victor Lecoffre, Paris. For the extracts from the Journals of the Margravine of Baireuth, the Editor is indebted to "The Memoirs of Frederica Sophia Wilhelmina, Princess Royal of Prussia and Margravine of Baireuth," published by Mr. Colburn in 1812. The chief biographical information concerning Miss Caroline Herschel consists of her Memoir by Mrs. John Herschel, and to that most interesting book indebtedness must be acknowledged.

Several of the lives mentioned have, during recent years, formed the subject of independent works; but a short record of them cannot be out of place in the annals of Noble Sisters.

Rydal Bank, Bradford,
    April, 1892.

CONTENTS.

	PAGE
Introductory	xi
"Sidney's Sister"	1
Wilhelmina, Margravine of Baireuth	47
Susanne Kossuth Meszlenyi	109
Caroline Lucretia Herschel	137
Dorothy Wordsworth	156
Mary Lamb	177
Elizabeth H. Whittier	211
Eugénie de Guérin	229

INTRODUCTORY.

WHILE the world abounds with records of noble lives—lives prominent in almost every station and department, thereby as examples affording stimulating incentive to high endeavour, there is one sphere of action which has, perhaps, not received due recognition—that of INFLUENCE. This moral force forms one of the most powerful factors in the development of character and the conduct of life. And whatever may be the varied opinions as to the political and civic rights of women, it cannot be doubted that they have a mission in the world, and that a mighty one. This province of influence is peculiarly their own, quite irrespective of age or degree, and is absolutely limitless in its power and extent. Where we may endeavour to drive or even to lead in vain, influence, with subtle tact and potent sway, may, like a gracious Divinity, become an unseen but pervading power, restoring, controlling, directing those who come within her realm. And while the gentler sex exercise this sovereign dominion more especially in the familiar arena of Home, where each affinity affords its own occasion for the exercise of that form of power befitting those who come into contact with each other, no relation in life can be greater in opportunity for beneficial influence, or need be richer in result, than that arising from the sweet bond existing between brother and sister. The natural tie, strengthened by the companionships of rosy childhood, cemented during years of youthful growth, prepares a fitting soil for life's seed-time, fit subjects for affection's persuasive sway. Each stage of their undivided lives adds to that store of mutual memories and loves, which gives to after life such a charm, importing therein "The cloistered memories of youth."

Approaching thus her womanhood, a girl having brothers to whom she is thus bound by the sanctities of the home life, has their future weal in no small measure within her power.

Unusual talent, if not genius, is frequently found to have distinguished various members of a family. The reason is not always to be found in heredity. Where one has early shown an aptitude for a particular pursuit, or become absorbed in a certain mental recreation, a brother or a sister, animated in the first place by love, has become interested in the other's work. From sympathy they pass to mutual labour. The worker is stimulated and helped, and love itself is strengthened. Kindred aim leads to kindred thought, oneness of purpose to oneness of heart. Each acts as an aid to the other.

> Their work becomes the better for their love,
> And still their love the sweeter for their work.

The following sketches of exalted sisterhood are gleanings only, and are offered as examples not heroic, but for the most part capable of emulation. Probably many other instances, kindred in character, will occur to those who may read these pages. We remember from the remote past the tragic story of Antigone, a maiden of heroic devotion, not only as daughter but sister. How, following her father in his sightless-age, she ministered to him until the end. And when, after the battle in which she had the anguish of seeing her brothers fighting against each other to the death, each falling by the hand which should have been the first to protect, the sister's heart yearned over the one left unburied. The victorious army had removed for decent burial those who had fallen on their side, but a tyrant king had forbidden, on pain of death, the burial of Polynices. But Antigone had a love which overcame all fear. Memories of mutual affection in days of innocence thronged her thought, and steeled her heart to defiance of the cruel law. Undeterred by the thought of how uncertain it was whether she could find her brother on the vast field, or that she would probably be discovered, and herself fall a victim to the passions of war; drawn by her mighty love, she dared alone the unknown and midnight horrors of the place of carnage, in the hope of hiding the loved body from the beasts of prey. After much search she came upon the dear object of her daring, and made in the ground a little space to serve her end. We should have liked to read that love so devoted met with its proper recompense. But, alas! Antigone was discovered and ordered to be confined in a subterranean cavern; when, no longer desiring to live, she died by her own hand.

An affecting incident of more recent days is recorded of Mdlle. Gattey, the sister of a bookseller who had been arrested during the French Revolution. The devoted sister determined to share the fate of her brother, whatever it might be. She was present on the occasion of his trial, apparently an indifferent spectator. When she heard the sentence of death pronounced against him, eager to become his companion to the scaffold, she shouted aloud: "Vive le Roi!" She was, of course, immediately taken, and, though not allowed to die with her brother, as her loving heart longed, she willingly shared his fate on the following day.

We need not, however, look into the past, nor so much at the fields of history as that of our own memories. Even the examples selected for our study have not been, for the most part, in the world's sense heroines, but rather sweet household women, doing the work which God placed nearest to them. They are not, therefore, any the less noble examplars; rather more. The common nature of humanity is not of heroic mould, nor are everyday needs such as demand its display. The restoration and salvation, the continual wellbeing and upraising of humanity depend not upon the extraordinary so much as upon the continuous exercise of those qualities which are our common heritage. In the army of helpers the best results are not attained by great endeavours so much as by the humble ministries which wait for the willing hands and kind hearts.

It may be that reading these pages the shadow of a cloud may flit over the thoughtful face of some sister, who, with a glowing feeling of affection, thinks with regret on what may appear to be a narrow sphere. If so, let it be remembered that lives are no less noble for being less known. Happily in many walks of life—lowlier in the fact that their events are unrecorded—beat hearts as warm, and in more limited spheres live deeds as noble and shine influences as pure and strong as those which, through the brighter light of exalted position or conspicuous circumstance, have added to the world's best wealth.

"SIDNEY'S SISTER."

"SIDNEY'S SISTER."

> "They had been taught religion—thence
> Their gentler spirits suck'd sweet innocence:
> Each morn and even they were taught to pray
> With the whole household; and could every day
> Read in their virtuous parents' noble parts.
> The mysteries of manners, morals, arts."
> BEN JONSON.

AMONG the examples of noble Sister-hood, a prominent place must be given to the illustrious lady remembered by the above designation, Mary Sidney, afterwards Countess of Pembroke. Whether we have regard to her sweetness of disposition, her piety, her lofty and cultured intellect, her devotion to duty, or her singularly close attachment to her famous brother, her life is one of great interest. A few threads of it may be fittingly woven together, prominence being given to her character of Sister.

She was born in a famous age, of a noble stock. It has been observed that "no period of the English history is more richly adorned with examples of genuine worth, than the golden age of Queen Elizabeth. It was an age of reviving literature, when men began to be esteemed according to their wisdom."

Mary Sidney was the daughter of Sir Henry Sidney, Lord Deputy of Ireland and Lord President of Wales, who had married Lady Mary, eldest daughter of John, Duke of Northumberland, who was, along with his son, Lord Guilford Dudley, beheaded for devotion to the cause of the noble, but ill-fated, Lady Jane Grey.

In such parentage Mary Sidney could not but be blessed. Her father had been the close friend and companion of the youthful King, Edward VI., who had expired in his arms. He appears to have been as distinguished for his learning as for the virtues which marked his private life, and the rectitude which characterised the discharge of his public duties. Of the mother of Mary Sidney it has been said that "she was not less distinguished in her sphere; one indeed, if not of equal splendour and publicity with that in which her husband moved, yet to her children, and, through her example to the world at large, no less useful and honourable; for with abilities every way adequate to the task of instruction, and with a devotedness and sense of duty which rendered her exertions a never-failing source of gratification and delight, she gave up her time almost exclusively to the early education of her offspring, superintending not only their initiation into the principles of religion and virtue, but directing their studies, and regulating, and even partaking in, their sports and relaxations."

Mary Sidney was born in or about the year 1557, at the historic castle of Penshurst, in Kent. It had been granted by King Edward VI. to Sir William Sidney, the grandfather of Mary. Ben Jonson has left a pleasant description of Mary's birth-place, in reference to which he says :—

"Thou art not, Penshurst, built to envious show
Of touch or marble, nor canst boast a row
Of polished pillars or a roof of gold:
Thou hast no lantern whereof tales are told;
Or stair, or courts; but standst an ancient pile;
And these, grudged at, are reverenced the while.
Thou joy'st in better marks of soil and air,
Of wood, of water; therein art thou fair.
Thou hast thy walks for health as well as sport
Thy mount, to which thy dryads do resort,

> Where Pan and Bacchus their high feasts have made,
> Beneath the broad beech and the chestnut shade;
> That taller tree, which of a nut was set,
> At his great birth where all the muses met;
> There, in the writhèd bark, are cut the names
> Of many a Sylvan taken with his flames;
> And there the ruddy satyrs oft provoke
> The lighter fauns to reach thy lady's oak."

Mary Sidney was two or three years younger than her brother Philip, to whom she became such a loving and devoted companion, and upon whose character and life she exercised such a powerful influence. Being a child of rare natural endowments, it can be well understood that, brought up in such a home, and under the immediate care of such parents, who appreciated learning at its true value and for its own sake, she early exhibited those charms and accomplishments which rendered her conspicuous among the learned, and her society courted by the greatest of that brilliant age. In all probability her early training was conducted side by side with that of her brother Philip. With minds and dispositions cast in similar moulds, kindred influences began early to work towards the formation of their young lives. Learning the same lessons, reading the same books, and with the like wise and loving counsels instilled into their receptive minds, they grew up with only such loving rivalry as tended to stimulate their exertions and cement their friendship. We can imagine how, their youthful tasks performed, they would wander forth hand-in-hand in the grounds of Penshurst, making the ancient woods ring with their merry laughter. Or, sauntering by the waters of the Medway, would, after the manner of thoughtful children, speculate on the future, weaving bright dreams of happiness in store, and making vows of eternal friendship.

We have some knowledge of how well Philip and his sister availed themselves of the advantages conferred upon them by the self-denying devotion of their mother. Her example is, in its results, full of encouragement to those parents who, having the ability, find also the opportunity of personally instructing their young children. It has been said that "English history can scarcely show two characters more thoroughly good and amiable than were Philip Sidney and his sister." We do not gather grapes where thorns have been sown. There is yet something to be learnt from the example of the Hebrew mothers, who had the sole charge of their children until they were five years old. Even then the girls remained the especial care of their mother, who still continued also to take part in the education of the boys. We find King Lemuel paying a tribute of filial remembrance in, after many years, recording the words "that his mother taught" him.

At the age of about twelve years, however, Philip was sent to school at Shrewsbury. It was about this time that his father, so impressed with the beauty of his disposition and the zeal he displayed for learning, styled him *Lumen familiae sue*—the ornament of his family. A letter written by Sir Henry to his son affords a pleasant insight into the character of the writer, and embodies advice which would adorn any page. The following is an extract:—

"Since this is my first letter that ever I did write to you, I will not that it be all empty of some advices, which my natural care of you provoketh me to wish you to follow. Let your first action be the lifting up of your mind to Almighty God by hearty prayer; and feelingly digest the words you speak in prayer, with continual meditation and thinking of Him to whom you pray and of the matter for which you pray. And use this as an ordinary act, and at an ordinary hour. Whereby the time itself will put you in remembrance to do that which you are accustomed to do in that time. Apply your study to such hours as your discreet master doth assign you, earnestly; and the time I know he will so limit as shall be both sufficient for your learning and for your health. And mark the sense and the matter of that you read, as well as the words; so shall you both enrich your tongue with words and your wit with matter; and judgment will grow as years grow in you. Be humble and obedient to your master, for unless you frame yourself to obey others, yea, and feel in yourself what obedience is, you shall never be able to teach others how to obey you. . . . Give yourself to be merry, for you degenerate from your father if you do not find yourself most able in wit and body and to do anything when you be most merry; but let your mirth be ever void of all scurrility and biting words to any man, for a wound given by a word is oftentimes harder to be cured than that which is given with the sword. . . . Think upon every word that you will speak before you utter it, and remember how Nature hath ramparted up, as it were, the tongue with teeth, lips, yea, and hair without the lips, and all betokening reins or bridles for the loose use of that member. Above all things, tell no untruth; no, not in trifles; the custom of it is naughty. And let it not satisfy you that, for a time, the hearers take it for truth; for after it will be known as it is, to your shame; for there cannot be a greater reproach to a gentleman than to be counted a liar. Study and endeavour yourself to be virtuously occupied; so shall you make such a habit of well-doing in you that you shall not know how to do evil though you would."

To this letter the Lady Mary wrote a postscript full of wise and tender sympathy, in which she speaks of her desire that God shall plant in him His grace, and advises him to read over every four or five days the "excellent counsels" of his father.

It is needless to say how well young Philip appreciated and availed himself of the advice of his wise parents and the opportunities afforded him of advancement. During the time of his stay at Shrewsbury the official duties of his father as Lord President of the Marches of Wales necessitated his residence at Ludlow Castle, where Philip would have many opportunities of visiting and of enjoying the society of his beloved sister.

At an early age Philip went to Oxford, and subsequently to Cambridge. His reputation for learning at the former University was such that his tutor, Dr. Thomas Thornton, himself a man of remarkable learning, desired to have it recorded on his tomb that he had been the tutor of Sir Philip Sidney when at Oxford.

After his distinguished career at the Universities, Mr. Philip Sidney, wishing for the advantages to be gained by Continental residence and travel, applied to the Sovereign for permission. Accordingly, in 1572, we find him proceeding to visit various countries on the Continent. During this residence abroad so great was his reputation for learning and integrity, and so engaging his manners, that he formed lasting friendships with some of the most notable men of the age. Returning to England in May, 1575, Philip soon became one of the greatest ornaments and favourites of the brilliant Court of Queen Elizabeth, who showed him many tokens of her appreciation. Among other important trusts committed to him by his astute Sovereign was his appointment in 1576, when, it should be remembered, he was only twenty-two years of age, as Ambassador to the Court of the Emperor of Austria upon a mission requiring the exercise of considerable skill and judgment.

Meanwhile, Sidney's sister Mary grew up into bright and happy womanhood. The charms of her person were only equalled by the sweetness and amiability of her disposition, and the extraordinary culture of her mind. Among the many ladies of the time distinguished for their attainments Mary Sidney was prominent. The Queen herself set a worthy example. Having had for tutor the celebrated Roger Ascham, she had from her youth been devoted for learning, and herself spoke five languages. Her Court was adorned by the presence of many ladies of great distinction, but to Mary Sidney seems to have been awarded the palm, both for learning and true excellence of character. A portrait of her in

Lodge's 'Portraits of Illustrious Personages," from an original of Mark Gerard, representing her in her young womanhood, shows her to have been a person of an unusually gracious presence. The soft, wavy hair fringes a broad and high forehead, beneath which beams an eye soft and clear. The countenance is pleasing and expressive; the well-moulded and regular features present an appearance of repose and sweet thoughtfulness, which seem to bespeak the inward harmony of a well-balanced mind— the full, but not too prominent, lip ready to break into a smile. She appears, indeed, to have been gifted with that singular attractiveness, which in its compelling persuasiveness acts as a magnet. Some countenances there are which the thoughts and affections of years have carved and moulded into a beauty which reveals the heart to be full of human tenderness. Such were the Sidneys. Mary closely resembled her brother, not only in mind, but also in feature. Spenser speaks of her as

> The gentlest shepherdess that lives this day,
> And most resembling both in shape and spright
> Her brother dear.

It is not the lapse of time only that has cast

a halo over this interesting pair. The most extravagant applause came from their contemporaries. Though some incidents of the life of Sidney himself reveal a hastiness of temper which show him to have been very far from perfection, he had at the same time such an equable combination of that nameless attractiveness of manner, which, with his virtues and attainments, made him admired and loved with an almost unequalled warmth, devotion, and constancy. While it has been said of Sidney that his "intemperance" (or hastiness) was the sole defect in his character, we do not find such a blemish in his sister. Beauty of feature and grace of manner did not in Mary Sidney complete the charm of contact, but only mirrored the indwelling soul, whence radiated

> The sweet, attractive kind of grace,
> A full assurance given by looks,
> Continual comfort in a face,
> The lineaments of Gospel books.

Before Mary Sidney was twenty years of age her hand was sought in marriage by Henry Herbert, Earl of Pembroke, to whom she was married in the year 1576. This match afforded considerable satisfaction to her father, as we see from a letter by him to his kinsman, the Earl of Leicester, whose good offices he was obliged to ask for the purpose of raising a dowry for his daughter. This letter rather painfully reminds us that it is not always the most deserving who, even in high places, receive their deserts. A servant less conscientious and faithful than Sir Henry would have found means of making his claims known, and would not have been allowed to endure the privations of poverty. After referring to the pleasure which the alliance would afford him, he says: "I have so joyfully at heart this happy advancement of my child that I would lie a year in prison rather than it should break. But, alas! my dearest lord, mine ability answereth not my hearty desire. I am poor; mine estate, as well in livelod and movable, is not unknown to your lordship, which wanteth much to make me able to equal that which I know my Lord of Pembroke may have. Two thousand pounds, I confess, I have bequeathed her, which your lordship knoweth I might better spare her when I were dead than one thousand living; and, in troth, my Lord, I have it not; but borrow it I must, and I will:

and if your Lordship will get me leave, that I may feed my eyes with that joyful sight of their coupling, I will give her a cup worth five hundred pounds. Good, my Lord, bear with my poverty; for, if I had it, little would I regret any sum of my own, but would willingly give it, protesting before Almighty God, that if He and all the powers on earth would give me my choice for a husband for her, I would choose the Earl of Pembroke."

The Earl of Leicester very generously provided his young kinswoman with a handsome dowry, and, the desired marriage taking place, Wilton House, the seat of the Pembrokes, thenceforth became the principal home of the young Countess.

The life of Mary Sidney had hitherto been one of influence rather than event. Her marriage did not tend to alter its character, so much as to widen its circle and extend its sphere. Exemplary and dutiful as a daughter, loving and helpful as a sister, she could hardly fail to be a devoted and faithful wife. Although her rank entitled her to a prominent place at Court, where she was ever a favourite, her inclination and tastes led her to prefer the retirement of the study, and the society of the learned rather than the great. If history is silent as to a large portion of her life, we may be sure it is a silence which speaks of "duties well performed and days well spent."

On the return of Mr. Philip Sidney from the Continent, in 1577, he made it one of his first duties to pay a visit to his sister in her new home, before entering more fully into public life, which his station and family interests demanded. It is, however, in his character as a scholar and patron of letters that he will be the most lovingly remembered. The friend of Raleigh, Spenser, Dyer, and others of not much less renown, it has been also said of him that "there was not a cunning painter, a skilful engineer, an excellent musician or any other artificer of extraordinary fame, that did not make himself known to this famous spirit, and found in him his true friend without hire."

A temporary retirement of Mr. Philip Sidney from Court in the year 1580, has been assigned to different causes. During the previous year the Duke of Anjou had so far pressed his suit for the hand of Elizabeth that she had shown an inclination to accept it. Opinions at Court were divided on the subject. Mr. Sidney, amongst others, was decidedly opposed to the alliance, as being likely to endanger the religious and civil liberty of the country. He had even the boldness to address to the Queen a strong, though courteous and elegant, remonstrance. To this some have attributed the fact that the negotiations for the match were broken off. It has been said that this action of Sidney did not give the smallest offence to the Queen; and that the reason for his subsequent early retirement is to be found in his quarrel with the Earl of Oxford. Others have fixed an earlier date for the last-named event, and trace the removal from Court to the resentment of the Queen at Sidney's interference with her proposed marriage. Whether Elizabeth openly resented the conduct of Sidney or not, she was hardly likely to forget it. The probability seems to be that the letter would arouse the secret indignation of the Queen, which only waited a suitable opportunity for showing itself. The opportunity arose for the Royal favour to be for a time withdrawn on the occasion of a misunderstanding between Sidney and the Earl of Oxford. In the early part of the last-mentioned year, however, Sidney retired from the Court, going to reside at the seat of his brother-in-law, the Earl of Pembroke. Here he regained the society of his beloved and like-minded sister; their happy intercourse was renewed, and mutual help afforded. In the solitudes of the Wilton Woods, at this time, their joint literary work was planned, and in great part performed. The extent of their mutual aid, and the exact part performed by each, will never be known. Although the whole of the beautiful romance, *The Arcadia*, is attributed to Philip, it is certain that his sister had no insignificant part in advising and directing it, so much so that he gave to it the name of " The Countess of Pembroke's Arcadia." The introduction is a pleasing record of their loving devotion and a testimony of fraternal gratitude :—

" TO MY DEAR LADY AND SISTER, THE COUNTESS OF PEMBROKE. Here have you now, most dear, and most worthy to be most dear,

Lady, this idle work of mine, which I fear, like a spider's web, will be thought fitter to be swept away than worn to any other purpose. For my part, in very truth, as the cruel fathers among the Greeks were wont to do to the babes they would not foster, I could well find in my heart to cast out in some desert of forgetfulness this child, which I am loath to father. But you desire me to do so; and your desire to my heart is an absolute commandment. Now it is done only for you, only to you. If you keep it to yourself, or to some friends who will weigh errors in the balance of goodwill, I hope for the father's sake it will be pardoned, perchance made much of, though in itself it have deformities; however, indeed for severer eyes it is not, being but a trifle, and that triflingly handled. Your dear self can best witness the manner, being done in loose sheets of paper, most of it in your presence, the rest by sheets sent to you as fast as they were done. . . . Read it, then, at your idle times, and the follies your good judgment will find in it blame not, but laugh at; and so, looking for no better stuff than, as in a haberdasher's shop, glasses or feathers, you will continue to love the writer, who doth exceedingly love you, and most, most heartily prays you may long live to be a principal ornament to the family of the Sidneys.

    Your loving Brother,
      PHILIP SIDNEY."

If the work was roughly completed by Philip, the duty remained for his sister, with loving melancholy, to revise and prepare it for the press after his death.

It appears to have been, also, at this time that Sidney and his sister commenced their joint work of translating the Psalms into English verse, to which it will be necessary to refer later.

Before alluding to the other literary labours of the Countess of Pembroke, reference may be made to the few remaining years of the life of her brother. Towards the close of the year we find him again at Court, and sitting in Parliament for his native county. Although holding the office of Cup Bearer to the Queen, he does not seem to have received any distinct marks of the Royal favour for some years. In fact, his family was neglected, and especially so his father, who had become impoverished through his disinterested devotion to the Crown. In the early part of 1583, however, Philip received from Her Majesty the honour of knighthood, together with benefits of a more substantial character. About the same time he married the daughter of the distinguished statesman, Sir Francis Walsingham.

It was about two years later, when Sir Philip was yet only in the flower of his manhood and the height of his fame, that he received the appointment which led to his early death. The President of the Netherlands, having applied to the English Queen for help against the Duke of Alva, she sent an expedition under the Earl of Leicester, Sir Philip being appointed General of the Horses and Governor of Flushing. Thither he repaired in the month of November, 1585, leaving his young and devoted wife (who had only shortly before given birth to a daughter) in England. In his character as a soldier, Sir Philip was as conscientious and brave as he was distinguished as a scholar and diplomatist; but he was not therein so happy. Entering with marked zeal and energy upon his duties, he conducted the campaign with considerable success in spite of many difficulties.

The year 1586 proved to be one of successive sorrows to the Countess of Pembroke. Her earliest affections had never waned. Blessed with such parents and brothers as she was, life without them could never be the same to her; and the rapidity with which the strokes of bereavement followed each other gave no room for Time's healing power to intervene. The first shock was sustained in the month of May by the death of her father. But three months later her mother finished her brave, devoted, and self-sacrificing life. However opinions may have differed as to her husband, no word seems to have been spoken or written of Lady Mary but in terms of the highest praise. "Born," says a competent authority, "of the noblest blood, surviving ambitious relatives who reached at royalty and perished, losing health and beauty in the service of an exacting Queen, suffering poverty at Court, supporting husband and children through all trials with wise counsel and sweet hopeful temper, she emerges with pale lustre from all the actors of that time to represent the perfect wife and mother in a lady of unpretending, but heroic, dignity." * This is the mother whom we find mirrored in her illustrious daughter.

This double bereavement, whilst her brother was still at Flushing, could not fail to have fallen heavily on the Countess. But this was not all. The close bonds which bound together brother and sister, not only in the most loving sympathy, but in interests and pursuits they both loved best, were destined to be rudely broken. Within two months came tidings of the disastrous events attending the siege of Zutphen and the scene of generous chivalry, which from its solitary grandeur has become familiar history. It was on the 22nd September, when Sir Philip was endeavouring to stop a reinforcement of the enemy on the way to Zutphen, that he received a wound in the thigh which subsequently proved fatal. He had displayed great valour, having twice had his horse shot under him and a third time returned to the charge. Here occurred the incident that, so well known, cannot be too often repeated.

* "Sir Philip Sidney." By J. A. Symonds, p. 180.

As Sir Philip was being taken from the field, weak and exhausted through loss of blood, he wished some water to be brought to him. As he was, however, in the act of raising the precious flask to his lips, his attention was drawn to a dying soldier, whose gaze was fixed longingly upon it. To this poor soldier he instantly handed the coveted beverage, saying, "Thy necessity is greater than mine."

As all the world knows, Sidney's wound proved fatal. After much suffering, borne with exemplary fortitude and resignation, he died in the arms of his faithful wife, who had joined him some time before, on the 7th October, 1586, while still only in the thirty-third year of his age. So greatly was his loss felt that the whole country went into mourning for him. His remains were brought to England and interred in St. Paul's Cathedral. It is said that no gentleman appeared in any gay or gaudy dress, either in the City or at the Court, for many months.

The poets and scholars of that cultured period vied with each other in speaking in praise of the departed. As he was so entirely one in heart with his twin-souled sister, the more immediate subject of this sketch, one of these may be selected by way of illustration. Camden, writing of him, says : "Philip Sidney, the great glory of his family, the great hopes of mankind, the most lively pattern of virtue, and the darling of the world, nobly engaging the enemy at Zutphen in Guelderland, lost his life bravely and valiantly. This is that Sidney whom, as Providence seems to have sent into the world to give the present age a specimen of the ancients, so did it on a sudden recall him, and snatch him from us, as more worthy of heaven than of earth. Thus when virtue has come to perfection it presently leaves us, and the best things are seldom lasting. Rest, then, in peace, O Sidney! if I may be allowed this address. We will not celebrate thy memory with tears, but with admiration. Whatever we loved best in thee (as the best of authors speaks of the best governor of Britain), whatever we admire in thee continues and will continue in the memories of men, the revolutions of ages, and the annals of time. Many, as being inglorious and ignoble, are buried in oblivion ; but Sidney shall live to all posterity.

For, as the Greek poet has it, Virtue is beyond the reach of fate."

An elegy, entitled, "The Doleful Lay of Clorinda," included by Spenser in his "Astrophel," and by him ascribed to the Countess of Pembroke, affords an example of her own writing and an intimation of the way in which she bore her irreparable loss. A few stanzas only can be quoted:—

"Ay me, to whom shall I my case complain,
   That may compassion my impatient grief?
Or where shall I unfold my inward pain,
   That my enriven heart may find relief?
     Shall I unto the heavenly powers it show,
     Or unto earthly men that dwell below?

    .   .   .   .   .

"Woods, hills, and rivers now are desolate,
   Sith he is gone the which did all them grace;
And all the fields do wail their widow state,
   Sith death their fairest flower did late deface.
     The fairest flower in field that ever grew,
     Was Astrophel; that was, we all may rue.

"What cruel hand of cursed foe unknown,
   Hath cropt the stalk that bore so fair a flower?
Untimely cropt, before it well were grown,
   And clean defaced in untimely hour.
     Great loss to all that ever him did see;
     Great loss to all, but greatest loss to me!

"Ah! no; he is not dead, nor can he die;
But lives for aye in blissful Paradise.

. . . . .

"There liveth he in everlasting bliss,
　　Sweet spirit! never fearing more to die;
Nor dreading harm from any foes of his,
　　Nor fearing savage beasts' more cruelty.
　　　　Whilst we here, wretches, wail his private lack,
　　　　And with vain vows do often call him back."

Of the life of the Countess of Pembroke subsequently to the death of her brother there is not much to be gleaned. Her chief immediate care was to complete and prepare for publication the manuscripts left by him. This labour of love she doubtless found to be one of sweet melancholy, which served, if anything could do, to endear still more his memory. It is stated that Sir Philip, on his death-bed, expressed a desire that the *Arcadia* should be committed to the flames. But, with a greater regard for his reputation than a simple compliance with his desire would have evinced, his sister lovingly undertook the task of revising, correcting, and completing this work. How much we are indebted to the pruning and shaping of the gentler hand we do not know. She carefully removed all blemishes, which, though not uncommon in the literature of the time, could not but offend her more refined sense of delicacy. It is, indeed, probable that the share of the sister in the romance is much larger than has been commonly supposed. In an address prefixed to some earlier editions it is said : " It moved that noble lady, to whose honour consecrated, to whose protection it was committed, to take in hand the wiping away those spots wherewith the beauties thereof were unworthily blemished. But as often repairing a ruinous house, the mending of some old part occasioneth the making of some new, so here her honourable labour began in correcting the faults, indeed in supplying the defects ; by view of what was ill done, guided to the consideration of what was not done. Which part, with what advice entered into, most by her doing, all by her directing, if they may be entreated not to divine, which are unfurnished of means to discern, the rest, it is hoped, will favourably censure." " It is now," adds the writer, " by more than one interest, the Countess of Pembroke's ' Arcadia,' done, as it was, for her, as it is, by her. Neither shall these pains be the last (if no unexpected accident cut off her determination) which the everlasting love of her excellent brother will make her consecrate to his memory."

The "Arcadia" was, according with the intention thus expressed, not the only memorial of the loving sympathy of the Countess of Pembroke and her brother. In addition to their joint translation of the Psalter, Sir Philip, at the time of his death, had almost completed a translation from the French of a work by his friend Philip de Mornay Du Plessis on "The True Use of the Christian Religion." This was completed and published a few months after the death of Sir Philip. The intimacy of her brother with Du Plessis doubtless induced the Countess also to study his works, which so much commended themselves to her that, some years later, she translated and published "A Discourse of Life and Death." The following passage from the preface, written by the Countess, affords a pleasant illustration of her prose writings, and at the same time is strikingly suggestive of her thoughtful character:—

"It seems to me strange," she writes, "and a thing much to be marvelled, that the labourer to repose himself hasteneth, as it were, the course of the sun; that the mariner rows with all his force to attain the port, and with a joyful cry salutes the descried land; that the traveller is never quiet nor content till he be at the end of his voyage; and that we in the meanwhile, tied in this world to a perpetual task, tost with continual tempest, tired with a rough and cumbersome way, cannot yet see the end of our labour but with grief, nor behold our port but with tears, nor approach our home and quiet abode but with horror and trembling. This life is but a Penelope's web, wherein we are always doing and undoing; a sea open to all winds, which, sometime within, sometime without, never cease to torment us; a weary journey through extreme heats and colds, over high mountains, steep rocks and thievish deserts. And so we term it, in weaving this web, in rowing at this oar, in passing this miserable way. Yet, lo! when Death comes to end our work; when she stretcheth out her arms to pull us into port; when, after so many dangerous passages and loathsome lodgings, she would conduct us to our true home and resting-place; instead of rejoicing at the end of our labour, of taking comfort at the sight of our land, of singing at the approach of our happy mansion, we would fain (who would believe it?) retake our work in hand, we would again hoist sail to the wind, and willingly undertake our journey anew. No more then remember we our pains; our shipwrecks and dangers are forgotten; we fear no more the travails and the thieves. Contrariwise, we apprehend death as an extreme pain, we doubt it as a rock, we fly it as a thief. We do as little children, who all the day complain, and when the medicine is brought them, are no longer sick; as they who all the week long run up and down the streets with pain of the teeth, and, seeing the barber coming to pull them out, feel no more pain. We fear more the cure than the disease, the surgeon than the pain. We have more sense of the medicine's bitterness, soon gone, than of a bitter languishing, long continued; more feeling of death, the end of our miseries, than the endless misery of our life, and wish for that we ought to fear."

The literary labours of the Countess of Pembroke were not, however, confined to prose. The work by which she is most deservedly remembered as a writer was the unique translation of the Book of Psalms, begun during the latter part of the life of Sir Philip, and completed by his sister after his death. This work is interesting not only as a joint production, the result of a loving unity of thought and pursuit, but also from its remarkable character. It bears at once the stamp of serious thought, scholarship, and rare culture. Composed of various kinds of verse, to suit best the subject and scope of the Psalm, it contains passages of striking power and beauty. It does not seem to be settled with absolute certainty which portions were written by Sir Philip and which by his sister. Unfortunately, the original manuscript, which was for many years preserved in the library at Wilton House, appears to have been lost. Probably the earlier portions were, if written by the brother, so written while he was enjoying much of his sister's society, either at Wilton or at the old residence overlooking Coniston Lake, in which the Countess for a period resided, and whither Sir Philip would come riding over the hills to visit her. The editor of the Chiswick Press edition, issued in 1823, in referring to the various MS. copies in existence, gives a substantial reason for endorsing the opinion of Dr. Woodford, a contemporary of the Sidneys, that the earlier part, as far as the 43rd Psalm, was the work of Sir Philip, and the remainder, much the greater portion, by the sister. Mr. Ruskin has done excellent service in publishing in his "Bibliotheca Pastorum" portions of the first half of the work. He has stated that, in commencing, he had expected to have little difficulty in distinguishing Sidney's work from that of any other writer concerned in the book. "But," he says, "I found, with greater surprise, that, instead of shining out with any recognisable brightness, the translations attributed by tradition to Sidney included many of the feeblest in the volume; and that, while several curious transitions in manner, and occasional fillings and retouchings by evidently inferior writers, were traceable through the rest, the entire body of the series was still animated by the same healthy and impetuous spirit, and could by no criticism of mine be divided into worthy and unworthy portions." This significant and authoritative criticism, however, only strengthens the assumption that the greater portion, and the best, is the work of the sister. There is no reason to suppose that her power as a writer or skill as a versifier was inferior to that of her brother. The objection advanced by some, that she would not be likely to have had the requisite knowledge of Hebrew to undertake such a work, is even of less importance. The period was remarkable for female learning. Her kinswoman, Lady Jane Grey, is said by Sir Thomas Chaloner, a contemporary, to have been well versed in Hebrew, Chaldee, Arabic, French, and Italian, in addition to Greek and Latin; and, remembering the disposition and pursuits of the Countess, it is not at all improbable that she possessed the necessary learning for the important work attributed to her. Daniel, also a poet of the period, referring to this version of the Psalms, says :—

"By this, great lady, thou must then be known,
When Wilton lies low levelled in the ground;
And this is that which thou must call thine own,
Which sacrilegious time cannot confound;
Here thou survivest those; here thou art found
Of late succeeding ages, fresh in fame,
Where in eternal brass remains thy name."

It is also a noticeable fact that in a portrait of the Countess, a copy of which is prefixed to the edition before mentioned, the lady is taken holding in her hand a copy of " David's Psalmes."

We cannot do more than give a few passages of this exquisite work of Mary Sidney. They will serve to show how carefully the subject had been studied, having regard to the circumstances, the mind and purposes of the psalmist, and how the meaning and beauty are elaborated and emphasized.

Psalm 72.

Teach the king's son, who king himself shall be,
   Thy judgments, Lord; thy justice make him learn :
To rule thy realms as justice shall decree,
   And poor men's rights in judgment to discern.
      Then fearless peace
      With rich increase
      The mountains proud shall fill ;
      And justice shall
      Make plenty fall
      On ev'ry humble hill.

Make him the weak support, th' oppressed relieve,
   Supply the poor, the quarrel-pickers quail :
So endless ages shall Thee reverence give,
   Till eyes of heav'n, the sun and moon, shall fail.
      And Thou again,
      Shall blessings rain,

Which down shall mildly flow,
As showers thrown
On meads new-mown,
Whereby they freshly grow.

During his rule the just shall aye be green,
  And peaceful plenty join with plenteous peace;
While of sad night the many-formèd queen
  Decreased shall grow, and grown, again decrease.
From sea to sea
He shall survey
All kingdoms as his own;
And from the trace
Of Perah's race,
As far as land is known.

The desert-dwellers at his beck shall bend,
  His foes then suppliant at his feet shall fling,
The kings of Tharsis homage-gifts shall send;
  So Seba, Saba, ev'ry island king.
Nay all, ev'n all,
Shall prostrate fall,
That crowns and sceptres wear:
And all that stand
At their command,
That crowns and sceptres bear.

For he shall hear the poor when they complain,
  And lend them help, who helpless are oppress'd:
His mercy shall the needy sort sustain;
  His force shall free their lives that live distress'd.
From hidden sleight,
From open might,
He shall their souls redeem:

His tender eyes
Shall highly prize,
And dear their blood esteem.

So shall he long, so shall he happy live;
　Health shall abound, and wealth shall never want:
They gold to him, Arabia gold, shall give,
　Which scantness dear, and dearness maketh scant.
They still shall pray
That still he may
So live, and flourish so:
Without his praise,
No nights, no days,
Shall passport have to go.

Look how the woods, whose interlacèd trees,
　Spread friendly arms each other to embrace,
Join at the head, though distant at the knees,
　Waving with wind, and lording on the place;
So woods of corn
By mountains borne
Shall on their shoulders wave:
And men shall pass
The numerous grass,
Such store each town shall have.

Look how the sun, so shall his name remain;
　As that in light, so this in glory one:
All glories this, as that all lights shall stain:
　Nor that shall fail, nor this be overthrown.
The dwellers all
Of earthly ball
In him shall hold them blest:

As one that is
Of perfect bliss,
A pattern to the rest.

O God who art—from whom all beings be;
Eternal Lord, whom Jacob's stock adore,
And wondrous works are done by only Thee,
Blessed be Thou, most blessed evermore.
    And let Thy name,
    Thy glorious fame,
No end of blessing know:
    Let all this round
    Thy honour sound,
So Lord, O be it so!

Psalm 139.

O Lord, in me there lieth naught,
  But to Thy search revealèd lies:
    For when I sit
    Thou markest it:
No less than notest when I rise.
Yea, closest closet of my thought
  Hath open windows to Thine eyes.

Thou walkest with me when I walk,
  When to my bed for rest I go,
    I find Thee there,
    And everywhere;
Not youngest thought, in me doth grow,
No, not one word I cast to talk,
  But yet unuttered, Thou dost know.

If forth I march, Thou goest before;
If back I turn, Thou comest behind
   So forth nor back
   Thy guard I lack,
Nay, on me, too, Thy hand I find.
Well I Thy wisdom may adore,
But never reach with earthly mind.

To shun Thy notice, leave Thine eye,
  Oh, whither might I take my way?
   To starry sphere?
   Thy Throne is there.
To dead men's undelightsome stay?
There is Thy walk, and there to lie
Unknown, in vain I should essay.

O Sun, whom light nor flight can match,
  Suppose thy lightful, flightful wings
   Thou lend to me,
   And I could flee
As far as thee the evening brings:
Even led to West, He would me catch,
  Nor could I lurk with Western things.

Do thou thy best, O secret Night,
  In sable veil to cover me;
   Thy sable veil
   Shall vainly fail:
With day unmasked my night shall be,
For night is day, and darkness light,
  O Father of all Lights, to Thee.

While this brilliant translation of the Book of Psalms would itself have sufficed to have made the reputation of the Countess of Pembroke as a scholar and poet, her poetical work was not limited thereto. We have also from her pen: "The Tragedie of Antonie: done into English by the Countess of Pembroke," published 1595, and a "Pastoral dialogue in praise of Astrea," published in Davidson's "Poetical Rapsody," in 1662, which is stated to have been made on the occasion of a visit being paid by the Queen at the house of the Countess.

This learned lady also left in manuscript a poem of considerable length entitled, "The Countess of Pembroke's Passion." It is only during the present century that this work has been given to the world. The poem is a touching lamentation over the sufferings of the Saviour. The subject itself, and the way in which it is handled, show how thoroughly the mind of the writer was impregnated with religious thought, and her ever ready and tender sympathy. It is a poem of very unequal merit, but some stanzas are sweet. Take the following:—

He placed all rust, and had no resting place;
  He healed each pain, yet lived in sore distress;

Deserved all good, yet lived in great disgrace;
  Gave all hearts joy, himself in heaviness;
    Suffered them live, by whom himself was slain:
    Lord, who can live to see such love again?

* * * * * *

Where He that sits on the supernal throne,
  In majesty most glorious to behold,
And holds the sceptre of the world alone,
  Hath not his garments of imbroidered gold,
    But he is clothed with truth and righteousness;
    Where angels all do sing with joyfulness.

Where heavenly love is cause of holy life,
  And holy life increaseth heavenly love;
Where peace established without fear or strife,
  Doth prove the blessing of the soul's behove;
    Where thirst nor hunger, grief nor sorrow dwelleth
    Put peace in joy, and joy in peace excelleth.

The Countess of Pembroke was, throughout her life, an unselfish and generous patron of letters. The noble old library at famous Wilton was collected chiefly during her residence there. The poets of the time seem to have vied with each other in speaking her praise, and in bearing testimony to her learning and rare excellence of character. Although it may be said that to some extent the many warm eulogies passed upon her came from interested sources, and are of too flattering a character to be invariably sincere, the lady whose virtues and worth were so warmly and universally sung must have been of nobly-souled and exalted nature. Churchyard, Daniel, Smart, and others of the period, are not alone in their plaudits. None was more enthusiastic than Spenser himself. His references to her are not solitary. The following in " Colin Clout's come home again " may be mentioned :—

> They all [quoth he] me gracèd goodly well,
> That all I praise : but in the highest place,
> Urania, sister unto Astrophell,
> In whose brave mind, as in a golden coffer,
> All heavenly gifts and riches lockèd are ;
> More rich than pearls of Ind, or gold of Ophir,
> And in her sex more wonderful and rare.

Her age was no less honoured than her youth. It has been said of her that " when an old woman she could entrance the world by her sweet beauty of her face, the gentleness of her womanly heart, the strength and keenness of her wit, and the depth and breadth of her learning." Her husband died in the month of January, 1602. She survived him twenty years. By the marriage there were three children—William, Philip, and a daughter named Anne, who died young. William, who on the death of his father became Earl of Pembroke, was, according to Clarendon, the most universally beloved and esteemed of any man of that age. He is believed by some to have been the "W. H." of Shakespeare's Sonnets, of whom that poet says:—

> Thou art thy mother's glass, and she in thee
> Calls back the lovely April of her prime.

From the second son, Philip, who succeeded his elder brother to the title, the present Earl of Pembroke is descended.

After having most truly lived her long life—a life faithful, devoted, and true—the Countess of Pembroke died at her town house in Aldersgate Street, on the 25th September, 1621. She was interred in the vault of her husband's family in Salisbury Cathedral.

A noble life is its own monument. To have influenced such a life as that of Philip Sidney; to have lived her own life—with its lasting impress on the literature of England, and its beneficial lessons to England's daughters—is to the subject of this sketch a more worthy and lasting memorial than stateliest pile of finest marble. We are, nevertheless, thankful for the familiar words of Ben Jonson :—

> Underneath this sable hearse
> Lies the subject of all verse,
> Sidney's sister, Pembroke's mother.
> Death, ere thou hast killed another,
> Fair and learned, and good as she,
> Time shall throw a dart at thee.

WILHELMINA, MARGRAVINE OF BAIREUTH.

WILHELMINA, MARGRAVINE OF BAIREUTH.

*His sorrow was my sorrow, and his joy
Sent little leaps and laughs thro' all my frame.*

WILHELMINA, the beloved and devoted Sister of Frederick the Great, will be remembered chiefly as such, although her high character in other respects, and her chequered and saddened life, render it one of no common interest.

To her immediate parentage she owed little; and, as is so frequently the case, we must attribute her excellences to a remoter ancestry. Her father, the then Prince Royal, afterwards Frederick William of Prussia, at no period of his life seems to have been possessed of any qualities of either mind or heart which "become the throned monarch better than his crown," or are of a truly kingly character. It was said of him by Macaulay that while "he must be allowed to have possessed some talents for administration," his "character was disfigured by odious vices, and his eccentricities were such as had never before been seen out of a madhouse."

While her father was harsh and cruel, her mother (a daughter of George I. of England) was scheming and selfish.

Wilhelmina Frederica Sophia was born on the 3rd July, 1709, and as her parents had looked for an heir, the royal infant had only an ungracious reception, and the presence of three sovereigns as sponsors at her baptism was a poor recompense for the love which ought to have been her portion.

Little Wilhelmina soon showed that she was a precocious child and possessed of more than ordinary intelligence. When she was three years old a little brother was born. This was Frederick (afterwards Frederick the Great) who became such a power in Europe, with whom her own life was destined to be so much associated, and to whom she became from childhood so passionately devoted.

The education of the young Princess was given into the hands of a lady who seems to have been well recommended to her parents, but was in no sense qualified for the post ; and the acquirements attained and good sense displayed by the pupil in after life, speak more for the qualities of her own mind and heart than for the care bestowed upon the choice of her associates.

In her Memoirs the Princess has mentioned a somewhat curious circumstance, which she takes care to state she considered only a coincidence. When she was about seven years old the Queen, her mother, sent for a Swedish astrologer, who was in Berlin, to tell the fortunes of herself and children. This astrologer foretold that Frederick would have a troubled youth, but that he would afterwards become one of the greatest princes that ever reigned, that he would make considerable acquisitions and die an Emperor. Of the Princess he said that her hand was not so lucky as that of her brother—that her life would be a tissue of fatalities, that she would be asked in marriage by four sovereigns, but would marry none of them. Singularly enough, the prediction was afterwards fulfilled.

Giving an account of her life at eight years old, she says: " All my time was taken up with my masters, and my only recreation was to see my brother. Never was affection equal to ours. His understanding was good, but his disposition gloomy. He was long considering before he returned an answer; but then his answers were just. He had great difficulty in learning, and it was expected that in time he would be more remarkable for good sense than for wit. My vivacity, on the contrary, was very great. I was prompt at repartee, and my memory was excellent. The King was passionately fond of me; he never paid so much attention to any of his children as to me. But my brother was odious to him, and never appeared before him but to be ill-used; this inspired the Prince Royal with an invincible fear of his father, which grew up with him —even to the age of maturity."

As she grew up, the childhood of Wilhelmina was sadly embittered by Court intrigues and home quarrels. State favourites plotting against the King, endeavoured to induce him, while she was yet quite a child, to engage his daughter in marriage in a certain direction. An ambitious mother, scheming in another, with the members of the Royal household acting as spies and go-betweens, did not augur well for the tranquillity and happiness of the Princess. Alternately caressed and snubbed, fondled and cuffed, Wilhelmina, young as she was, found her greatest pleasure in her studies and the society of her brother. It was she who first aroused him from indifference to intellectual pursuits, awakened in him a love of study, and stimulated his better nature. In this way they came to share each other's studies and recreations, and found in each other's presence mutual sympathy and consolation. To add to the misfortunes of Wilhelmina, she was shamefully ill-used and beaten by her governess, who wished, for purposes of her own, to induce her to disclose what passed between her father and mother. In consequence of this brutal treatment, Wilhelmina was from time to time seriously ill. Still Wilhelmina screened her governess, and it speaks well for her forgiving spirit that, when dismissal at last came, she deeply grieved for her, and sent her away loaded with costly presents.

Under a new governess, Madame von Sonsfeld, Wilhelmina's lot was much brighter. She says: " Madame de Sonsfeld began by studying my disposition. She observed that I was excessively timid. I trembled when she was very grave; I had not the heart to say two words together without hesitating. She represented to the Queen that it would be proper to divert me, and to treat me with much gentleness, to remove my fears; that I was extremely docile; and that, by exciting my ambition, she might do with me whatever she chose. The Queen left her complete mistress of my education. She every day reasoned with me about indifferent subjects, and endeavoured to inspire me with good sentiments on every occurrence. I applied myself to reading, which soon became my favourite occupation. The emulation which she excited in me made me relish my other studies. I learnt English, Italian, history, geography, philosophy, and music. My improvement was surprisingly rapid; I was so intent upon learning that Madame de Sonsfeld was obliged to moderate my ardour."

An incident showing her excellent memory, altogether remarkable in a child of thirteen, may be mentioned. A certain lady, Miss Polnitz, who was unfriendly towards Wilhelmina, had one day been speaking to the Queen about what she called her ungainly figure. " It is true," said the Queen, " that she might look better; but her shape is straight, and will display itself when she has done growing. However, if you converse with her, you will find that she is not a mere automaton." " Miss Polnitz," continues Wilhelmina, " thereupon began to talk with me, but in an ironical manner, asking me questions which would have suited a child of four years. I was so vexed that I did not deign to make any reply. My sullen behaviour gave her an opportunity to hint to the Queen that I was capricious and haughty, and that I had scrutinised her from head to foot. This brought upon me severe reprimands, which continued all the time Miss Polnitz stayed at Berlin. She quarrelled with me about everything. One day the conversation turned upon powers of memory. The Queen observed that I had an excellent memory. Miss Polnitz set up a malicious grin, as much as to say that she disputed the fact. The Queen, nettled at this, offered to try me, and proposed a wager that I could learn 150 verses by heart in an hour's time. 'Well,' said Miss Polnitz, 'I will try her local memory; and I will bet that she will not remember what I shall write down.' The Queen was consequently very strenuous to maintain what she had asserted, and I was sent for. Having taken me aside, the Queen told me she would freely forgive me all that was past if I proved successful, and so caused her to win her wager. I did not know what was meant by a local memory, having never heard of it before. Miss Polnitz wrote what I was to learn. It was a series of 150 fanciful names of her own invention, all numbered. She read them twice over to me, always mentioning the numbers; after which I was obliged to repeat them in succession. I was very fortunate in the first trial; she desired a second, and asked the names out of order, mentioning merely the number. I again succeeded, to her great vexation. I had never made a greater effort of memory; yet she could not prevail with herself to bestow upon me the slightest commendation. The Queen could not account for her behaviour, and was much offended, though she held her peace."

The situation of the Princess at this, as at all times, was one by no means to be envied.

By those from whom she ought to have received the most loving care she was misunderstood and neglected. Her health from time to time severely suffered. She had serious illnesses, which were disregarded by her mother, who, being herself strong and healthy, had no sympathy for those who were not so. Nor did her path become smoother as she grew older. The time seems to have been passed in schemes for her marriage, first to one Prince and then to another. The Queen had set her heart upon a double alliance with England by the marriage of Wilhelmina with the Prince of Wales, and of the Crown Prince Frederick with the Princess Amelia of England. She bent her energies for years to the accomplishment of this object, for which she seemed willing to sacrifice everything else. The King was willing, and at one time it appeared highly probable that it would be carried out. But the emissaries of Austria desired to prevent such an alliance between Prussia and England, and secretly sowed the seeds of dissension and jealousy in the Prussian household. Other marriages for Wilhelmina were suggested; first with the

King of Poland, and (when negotiations for this came to an end) afterwards with the Duke of Weissenfels. All these were quite regardless of her own inclinations and affections. Her views upon marriage differed from those of both her parents. She says:—"I maintain that a happy union ought to be founded upon mutual esteem and regard. I would have chosen reciprocal affection as its basis, and that my complaisances and attentions should flow from this source. Nothing appears difficult to us for those we love. . . . . . . I wished for a real friend, to whom I could feel both esteem and inclination; who might ensure my felicity; and whom I might render happy. I foresaw that the Prince of Wales would not suit me, as he did not possess the qualities which I required. The Duke of Weissenfels, on the other hand, pleased me still less. The state of my poor heart may easily be conjectured. There was no one but my governess who was acquainted with my real sentiments; and to none but her could I make them known."

Another source of ever-increasing anxiety with the Princess was her brother Frederick and his relations with the King. The Royal household was unfortunately a very unhappy one. Coarse and insufficient food only aggravated an unhappiness caused by the King's harsh and sometimes brutal treatment. Wilhelmina and her brother, in consequence of their having become the innocent cause of the King's disappointment, became the scapegoats of his unreasonable temper and violent fits of anger. Frederick grew moody and sullen, still further increasing his father's displeasure; while Wilhelmina's health became seriously impaired, and she was frequently alarmingly ill. Alluding to one of these illnesses, a fever which culminated in the smallpox, she writes: "In my short intervals of consciousness I ardently wished to die; and when I saw Madam de Sonsfeld and my good Mermann" [her old nurse] "weeping near my bed, I endeavoured to console them by telling them that I was weaned from the world, and that I was going to enjoy a repose which no one could disturb. I am, said I, the cause of both the Queen's and my brother's sorrows. If I am to die, tell the King that I have always loved him, that I have no fault to reproach myself with towards him; that therefore I hope he will give me his blessing before I quit this world. Tell him that I beseech him to treat the Queen and my brother more gently, and to bury all discontents and animosities against them in my grave. It is the only boon I wish him to grant me; and my only cause of uneasiness in my present state." During this illness she was deserted by every member of the Royal household but her brother, who went daily to spend with her what time he could spare.

The delays from time to time in the proposed betrothals, and the obstacles placed in the way by the secret intrigues of the representatives of Austria, considerably angered the King. He declared he would hear no more of the intended alliance, and gave the Princess the option of marrying the Duke of Weissenfels or the Margrave of Schwedt. To this the Queen, who had set her heart on the English alliance, would not consent. Wilhelmina, in this manner, gained time, stating that she desired, first of all, to see her father and mother agreed on the subject. Meanwhile the

King's ill-treatment of both Wilhelmina and her brother continued. She says: "The King starved my brother and myself: as he himself performed the office of carver, he helped every one at the table except us; and when by chance there was a bit left in any dish, he spat on it to prevent our tasting it. We lived on nothing but coffee and milk, and dried cherries, which entirely vitiated my stomach. My share of insult and invectives, on the contrary, was extremely liberal; the most abusive language was used towards me all the day, and in the presence of every one. The displeasure of the King was even carried to so great a length, that he ordered both my brother and myself never to appear in his presence but at the times of dinner and supper. He never saw my brother without threatening him with his cane. The Prince repeatedly told me that he would endure everything from his father except blows; and that if ever he proceeded to that extremity with him, he would withdraw from his power by flight."

Frederick was thus reduced to the necessity of meditating flight from the Court as a means of freeing himself from the continued cruelty of his father. In this state of mind he writes to his sister :

"I am still in the utmost despair; the tyranny of the King increases; my patience is exhausted. You vainly flatter yourself that the arrival of Sir —— Hotham will put an end to our sufferings. The Queen frustrates our plans by her blind confidence in Mrs. Ramen. The King is already informed through this woman of the news which are arrived, and the measures that are taken, at which he is more and more exasperated. I wish the old soul was hanged upon the highest gibbet; she is the cause of all our misfortunes. The Queen ought no longer to be made acquainted with any intelligence: her weakness for that infamous creature is unpardonable. The King will go to Berlin on Tuesday; it is still a secret. Adieu, my dear Sister, I am wholly Yours."

The anger of the King culminated on intelligence having come to his ears of the intention of Frederick to seek safety in flight. His fury knew no bounds. He used personal violence towards the Crown Prince, had him arrested and placed under restraint. So far did the madness go, that he was actually condemned to death along with a companion, Lieut. Katte, who was supposed to have been privy to his intentions. The sentence of Katte was executed before the eyes of Frederick, who was himself for many months kept a prisoner. Of Wilhelmina herself the King's treatment was hardly less severe. She says:—

"The King came back in the meantime. We all ran up to meet him to kiss his hands; but he had scarcely cast his eyes upon me, when anger and fury overpowered him. He grew black, his eyes sparkled with rage, and he foamed at the mouth. 'Infamous baggage!' said he to me, 'dare you show yourself before me? Go and keep company with your rascal brother.' In uttering these words, he seized me with one hand, and struck me several times in the face with his fist; one of his blows fell on my temples so violently, that I fell backwards, and should have split my head against the corner of the wainscot, had not Madam de Sonsfeld broken my fall by seizing me by my head-dress. The King, no longer master of himself, strove to renew the blows, and trample upon me; but the Queen, my brothers and sisters, and all who were present, prevented him. They all surrounded me; which gave Madam de Kamken and Madam de Sonsfeld time to lift me up. They placed me in a window-seat which was close by; but seeing that I continued senseless, they sent one of my sisters for a glass of water and some salts, with which they insensibly recalled me to life. As soon as I was able to speak, I reproached them for the pains which they took with me, death being a thousand times more agreeable than life in the situation in which we were. To describe its horror is impossible."

The devoted character of the friendship at this time existing between Wilhelmina and her brother is seen in the following letter which Frederick managed to get conveyed to her.

"My Dear Sister,—I am going to be declared a heretic by the Court Martial which is assembling, for not to conform in every respect to the sentiments of the master is enough to incur the guilty of heresy. You, therefore, may easily judge how prettily I shall be dealt with. I little care for the excommunication which will be thundered at me, provided I know that my amiable sister protests against it as unmerited. How sweet it is, that neither bars nor bolts can prevent my assuring you of my undiminished friendship! Yes, my dear sister, in this almost entirely perverted age, there are still means of expressing my affection for you. Yes, my dear sister, provided I know you are happy, my prison will be to me the abode of felicity and pleasure. *Chi ha tempo ha vita!* Let that comfort us. I heartily wish I may no longer need any interpreter to converse with you, and that we may see those happy days when your *principe* and my *principessa* [their flutes] will sweetly harmonize; or, to speak more plainly, when I shall have the pleasure to address you in person, and to assure you that nothing in the world can diminish my friendship for you. Adieu.

"THE PRISONER."

But the fury of the King was not yet abated. Wilhelmina herself was in great danger of becoming in a greater measure than heretofore the victim of his wrath. She gives the following account of an interview with a messenger of the King, who, on the 5th November, 1730, renewed the oft-repeated request that she would consent to marry one of the obnoxious princes. She says: "'The King,' I replied, 'is my master; he may dispose of my life, but he cannot render me guilty when I am innocent. I ardently wish to be examined; my innocence would then shine in all its splendour. With regard to the two proposed princes, they are both so hateful to me that it would be difficult to choose betwixt them; however, I shall submit to His Majesty's commands whenever he agrees with the Queen.' He set up a very insolent laugh. 'The Queen!' exclaimed he; 'the King has peremptorily declared that he will not suffer her to interfere in anything.' 'Yet he cannot prevent her continuing my mother, nor deprive her of the authority which that character gives her over me. How wretched is my fate! What occasion is there to marry me, and why do my parents not agree concerning the person whom I am to marry? My lot is most miserable; alternately threatened with the curses of my father and mother, I do not know what to resolve, as I cannot obey one without disobeying the other.'. 'Well, then,' continued Eversmann, 'prepare for death; I must no longer conceal anything from you. There is to be a second trial of the Prince Royal and Katte, in which you will be still more implicated. The King's wrath demands a victim; Katte alone will not suffice to extinguish his rage, and he will be glad to save your brother at your expense.' 'You delight me,' I exclaimed; 'I am weaned from the world; the adversities which I have experienced have taught me the vanity of all terrestrial things; I shall receive death with joy and without fear, since it will conduct me to a happy tranquillity, of which I cannot be deprived.' 'But what would then become of the Prince Royal?' continued Eversmann. 'If I can save his life my felicity will be complete; and if I die, I shall not feel the misery of surviving him.'"

The Princess was confined to her bedroom, where her only resource was reading. She was so deprived of necessary food that her health continued to suffer greatly, and she became almost as thin as a skeleton. She mentions a pathetic incident which occurred at this time. As she and her governess were one day seated at table contemplating ruefully their apology for a meal, consisting only of a kind of soup made of water and salt, and "a hash of stale bones, full of hair and filth," they heard a tapping at the window. Rising to ascertain the cause, they found it was a crow with a crust of bread in her bill, which she dropped on the window-ledge, and then flew away. "Our fate is lamentable indeed," said Wilhelmina to her companion, "since it moves even dumb creatures; they take more pity on us than human beings, who treat us with so much cruelty."

The Princess refers to the 6th May, 1731, as the most eventful day of her life. On that day messengers from the King waited upon her to renew the subject of her marriage, giving her the further option of marrying the Hereditary Prince of Baireuth, showing her at the same time an order for her imprisonment in case of her refusal, and offering, as a further inducement to her acquiescence, the liberty of her brother. On Wilhelmina again urging that she desired her father and mother to be of one mind on the subject, it was represented to her that the Queen would approve. In this dilemma, she consented to sacrifice her own inclinations, in the hope of restoring peace and goodwill in the family and, above all, gaining the pardon of her brother. Wilhelmina informed her mother of her resolution in the following letter:—

"MADAM,—Your Majesty is already acquainted with my misfortune by the letter which I had the honour to address to you yesterday under cover of the King. I have scarcely strength to trace these lines; my situation is entitled to commiseration. It is not the King's menaces, strong as they were, that have obtained my submission to the will of His Majesty; an interest more dear has determined me to the sacrifice. Hitherto I have been the innocent cause of the pains your Majesty has endured. My too feeling heart was violently affected at the picture your Majesty gave me of your troubles. My mother wished to suffer for me. Is it not more natural that I should sacrifice myself for her, and put a final stop to the fatal disunion of the family? Could I have hesitated a moment between my brother's misfortune and his pardon? What horrible projects have been disclosed to me in regard to him ! I shudder as I think of them. Whatever I could have advanced against the proposal of the King has been reflected on beforehand. You yourself have proposed the Prince of Baireuth as a suitable match for me, and you seemed satisfied if I married him ; I, therefore, cannot imagine that you will disapprove of my resolution. Necessity is a hard law ; all my entreaties for leave to obtain first the consent of your Majesty have been vain. I was forced to choose either to obey the King with a good grace, and obtain real advantages for my brother, or to expose myself to violence which in the end would still have reduced me to the measure which I have adopted. I shall have the honour to enter into a more minute account when I am allowed to embrace your Majesty's feet. Full well I feel how great must be your grief; it is that which affects me most. I humbly beseech your Majesty not to be disquieted on my behalf, and to rely on Providence, which does everything for our welfare ; particularly as I deem myself fortutunate in becoming the instrument of my dear mother's and brother's happiness. What would I not do to convince them of my affection! I once more entreat your Majesty to take care of your health, and not to impair it by immoderate sorrow. The prospect of seeing my brother soon must alleviate your Majesty's present misfortune. I hope your Majesty will generously forgive the fault I have committed of entering into any engagement unknown to your Majesty, in consideration of the tender regard and dutiful respect with which I shall remain for life, &c., &c."

It might have been thought that such a letter would have appealed to the better feelings of the Queen, and have aroused all her maternal sympathy. But not so. Although written in trembling anxiety as to the manner in which it might be received, probably Wilhelmina, with all her past experience of her mother's character, was not prepared for the Queen's reply. It was as follows:—" You break my heart by giving me the most violent pain I ever felt in my life. I had placed all my hopes in you; but I did not know you. You have artfully disguised the malice of your soul and the meanness of your sentiments. I repent a thousand times over the kindness I have had for you, the care I have taken of your education, and the torments I have endured for your sake. I no longer acknowledge you as my daughter, and shall henceforth consider you as my most cruel enemy, since it is you who sacrifice me to your prospects and triumph over me. I vow you eternal hatred, and never shall forgive you."

And Wilhelmina's mother never did forgive her. Her affection, ill-regulated and spasmodic as it had ever been, seems to have been withdrawn from her ill-fated daughter for the remainder of her life, only because she, against the dictates of her own heart and merely to propitiate her father and save her brother, at last consented to sacrifice herself by a marriage in which her own affections had not been consulted.

The Princess was, accordingly, married in November, 1731, when she was twenty-two years of age. Her beloved brother was set at liberty, and a few days afterwards she met him, after an absence of more than a year. As soon as she heard he was present at an assembly, she says :—" All my blood was in a paroxysm of joy. '.Oh, heavens! my brother!' I exclaimed; 'let me see him, for heaven's sake.' I leaped into his arms. I was so agitated that I uttered nothing but broken sentences. I wept; I laughed; looked like a person beside herself. Never in my life had I felt joy so lively. When my first emotion had subsided, I threw myself at the feet of the King, who said aloud, in my brother's hearing, 'Are you satisfied? You see that I have kept my word.' I took my brother by the hand and besought the King to admit him again to his favour. The scene was so affecting that it drew tears from the whole company." Wilhelmina, however, found her brother considerably changed and cold in his behaviour towards her. "I no longer," she says, "found in him that beloved brother who had cost me so many tears, and for whom I had sacrificed myself." She also writes:—" My brother had quite changed towards me since his return from the Rhine; a certain stiffness and embarrassment were visible in all his letters, which sufficiently showed that his heart was no longer the same. I felt this very keenly; my affection for him was not diminished, and I had nothing to reproach myself with. I bore all, however, with patience, flattering myself that I should one day recover his friendship."

Although Wilhelmina had no voice in arranging that most momentous step in her life, her own marriage, it proved happier than might have been expected. The Prince of Baireuth came much nearer answering to the standard she had formed as to what was desirable in a husband than any of the other suitors who had been forced upon her notice. Always faithful to her trust, she learned to love her husband with a devoted and constant affection. But her life was destined to be always stormy and tearful. The duties of her new position were trying and difficult, but she bore herself with dignity and patience amidst the trifling and intriguing jealousies of the two Courts. Her own marriage was quickly followed by that of her brother, brought about in his case also without the concurrence of his own inclination. The following is his letter announcing to her his engagement :—

"*Berlin, 6 March*, 1732.

"MY DEAR SISTER,—Next Monday comes my betrothal, which will be done just as yours was. The person in question is neither beautiful nor ugly, nor wanting for sense, but very ill brought up, timid, and totally behind in manners and social behaviour: that is the candid portrait of this Princess. You may judge by that, my dear sister, if I find her to my taste or not. The greatest merit she has is that she has procured me the liberty of writing to you; which is the one solace I have in your absence.

"You never can believe, my adorable sister, how concerned I am about your happiness; all my wishes centre there, and every moment of my life I form such wishes. You may see by this that I preserve still that sincere friendship which has united our hearts from our tenderest years; recognise at least, my dear sister, that you did me a sensible wrong when you suspected me of fickleness towards you, and believed false reports of my listening to talebearers—I, who love only you, and whom neither absence nor lying rumours could change in respect of you. At least, do not again believe such things on my score, and never mistrust me until you have had clear proof, or until God has forsaken me, and I have lost my wits. And, being persuaded that such miseries are not in store to overwhelm me, I here repeat how much I love you, and with what respect and sincere veneration, I am and shall be till death, my dearest sister, your most humble and faithful brother and valet,

"FREDERICK."

A short time afterwards in writing to her he says :—" God be praised that you are better, dearest sister, for nobody can love you more tenderly than I do. God long preserve you in perfect health! And you, keep for me always the honour of your good graces; and believe, my charming sister, that never brother in the world loved with such tenderness a sister so charming as mine; in short believe, dear sister, that without compliments, and in literal truth, I am, wholly yours."

That the brother and sister were still the first to each other is shown by their correspondence, the manner in which they always consulted each other, and kept each other informed of the incidents in each other's lives. On the morning of his marriage

Frederick writes to inform his sister of the event:—

"*Salzdalum, Noon, 12th June,* 1733.

"MY DEAR SISTER,—A minute since the whole ceremony was got finished, and, God be praised, it is over! I hope you will take it as a mark of my friendship that I give you the first news of it. I hope I shall have the honour to see you again soon, and to assure you, my dear sister, that I am wholly yours. I write in great haste, and do nothing that is merely formal. Adieu.

" FREDERICK."

For some years succeeding this period Wilhelmina and her brother do not seem, apart from their correspondence, to have had much personal intercourse. An important and interesting factor in their lives was their acquaintance and correspondence with Voltaire. This appears to date from the year 1736. Doubtless, during their youthful studies, pursued together years before, in spite of prohibition and difficulty, they had become acquainted with the writings of this great author. Now Frederick opened a correspondence, which, after continuing for four years, ripened into a closer acquaintance. They, however, never met until Frederick became King of Prussia. This event took place upon the death of his father, in May, 1740. In the month of November following Wilhelmina paid a memorable visit of several months to her brother, the King, at Rheinsburg, his stately and charming residence near Berlin, when he introduced Voltaire to her with the words, "I here present you to my loved sister." In connection with this visit we have the following pleasing picture:—" When evening comes, with the rough and chilly autumn air so common to that part of Germany, the candles are lit in the Queen's apartments, beautifully decorated by Pesne. The King, who has all day sat brooding over serious undertakings against the House of Hapsburg, now makes his appearance. The concert begins. The King leads the Margravine to the piano, and then takes his flute. During the pauses between the different pieces the Margravine holds philosophic and other discussions with Maupertis, Algarotti, Jordan, and Keyserling; but chiefly with Voltaire, whose society was so new, interesting, and invigorating."* The friendship thus formed, though Wilhelmina and Voltaire did not often meet, was continued by an interesting correspondence until the close of her troubled life.

Frederick, shortly after his accession to the throne, undertook the campaign against Austria, which when the other European Powers became involved, and there was arrayed against him perhaps the most powerful alliance ever formed, resulted in such disastrous wars, and for so many years disturbed the peace of Europe. How far the quarrel was justified, and whether the distinguished and eventful, and at the same time singular, career of Frederick as a King answered the high hopes formed of him, or proved for the common weal of his own country, are questions upon which varied opinions have been formed. It is now only fitting to trace slightly the passionate devotion and constant affection of the sister whose interest in his life and undertakings never waned. She never lost the refined and distinguished tastes of her

* "The Margravine of Baireuth and Voltaire." By Dr. George Horn. Translated by H.R.H. Princess Christian. p. 171.

youth, or abandoned the pursuit of literature and philosophy, and the cultivation of music. She was herself a proficient performer on several musical instruments, and found therein and in her love of learning a solace amidst the domestic troubles which came to embitter her life, and the enfeebled health in which it was passed. She set a brilliant example to her people. It has been said : "For twenty-three years the Court of a country numbering only 200,000 inhabitants rivalled those of other great countries in intellectual importance and renown. The Margravine was the magnet which attracted all that was greatest and most celebrated, all that was worthy of esteem and consideration."*

After the old Margrave's death her husband presented to her the Hermitage, a country residence near Baireuth, which she describes as a perfectly unique place, and as becoming under her directions one of the most beautiful castles in Germany. She gave much time and attention to its improvement, laying out the grounds and adding the most elaborate and beautiful works of art. It was at the Hermit-

---

* "The Margravine of Baireuth and Voltaire." p. 2.

age in the year 1744 that the Margravine wrote her celebrated Memorials, which form the chief authority for this account. These Memorials are deeply interesting and afford a striking picture of the Court life of the period. If the writer occasionally descends to coarseness or indelicacy, or speaks bitterly of her earliest years, or disrespectfully of her parents, we must remember the freedom of the time at which she wrote, the terrible hardships of her youth, her afflicted life, and still later, the loss of her husband's affections. On the whole she stands before us as a noble woman—the graceful and stately form, the beautifully modelled features, the dignified demeanour, befitting the possessor of the cultured mind, the kind heart, the constant and devoted life—faithful even to the death. It is to be regretted that the Margravine did not bring her Memorials down to a later period of her life. What remains of it is gleaned from her correspondence.

In his interludes of peace, as well as, indeed, during his many trying campaigns, Frederick devoted himself to the pursuit of literature. Stimulated by this devotion, as well as, doubtless, by a desire to add to the distinction of his Court and to his own character as a patron of letters, he induced the great French wit to take up his residence at the Castle at Potsdam. After the Treaty of Dresden, which closed the second great Silesian War and inaugurated a ten years' peace, the King added to his other residences his famous Garden Cottage, Sans-Souci. Here the literary monarch and the flattering courtier met and eulogised each other's productions. There is no doubt that Frederick here appears at his best. He was himself a voluminous writer, and it is much more pleasing to picture him in his retirement, writing history and poetry, however feeble, and receiving the plaudits of sycophants, than deluging the Continent with blood. Here, too, occasionally came Wilhelmina, renewing her acquaintance with the great *littérateur*, with whom she had much sympathy in common.

Voltaire's charmed life at Berlin was not, however, destined to be of long duration. After about two years the King seemed to grow weary of his intellectual favourite, and found excuses for cooling in his devotion. The circumstances under which Voltaire finally left Berlin were such that he, along with his niece, Madame Denis, were arrested, Voltaire himself only regaining his liberty after the lapse of a fortnight and on the mediation of the Margravine. This mutual friend endeavoured in vain to heal the breach between them. Although her own friendship with Voltaire was maintained during her life, the friendly character of the intercourse between him and her brother was never resumed.

But further troubles were in store for Frederick—troubles which were destined to try the nerves and break the heart of his devoted sister. When, in 1756, the war with Austria broke out again, the Margravine felt the keenest interest in it, and followed her brother's fortunes with aching heart. Intelligence of the brilliant successes which he gained and the terrible defeats sustained in his single-handed conflict with the four Powers who took up arms against him was forwarded by Frederick to his sister as opportunity offered, and fearful was the strain which her unchanging love was called upon to sustain during the last two years of her life. Here is a letter from the King to his sister, reporting progress :—

"*Leitmeritz, 13th July,* 1757.

"MY DEAREST SISTER,—The French have just laid hold of Friesland; are about to pass the Weser; they have instigated the Swedes to declare war against me; the Swedes are sending 17,000 men into Pommern; will be burthensome to Stralsund and the poor country-people mainly, having no captain over them but a hydra-headed National Palaver at home, and a Long-pole with cocked hat on it here at hand. The Russians have besieged Memel; Lehwald has them on his front and in his rear. The troops of the Reich, from your plain of Furth yonder, are also about to emerge. All this will force me to evacuate Bohemia so soon as that crowd of enemies gets into motion. I am firmly resolved on the extremest efforts to save my country. We shall see if Fortune will take a new thought, or if she will entirely turn her back upon me. Happy the moment when I took to training myself in philosophy! There is nothing else that can sustain the soul in a situation like mine. I spread out to you, dear sister, the detail of my sorrows; if these things regarded myself only I could stand it with composure; but I am bound guardian of the safety and happiness of a people which has been put under my charge. There lies the sting of it, and I shall have to reproach myself with every fault, if, by any delay or over-haste, I occasion the smallest accident; all the more as, at present, any fault may be capital.

"What a business! Here is the liberty of Germany, and that Protestant cause for which so much blood has been shed.; here are those two great interests again at stake, and the pinch of this huge game is such that an entirely unlucky quarter of an hour may establish over Germany the tyrannous dominion of the House of Austria for ever! I am in the case of a traveller who sees himself surrounded and ready to be assassinated by a troop of cut-throats who intend to share his spoils. Since the League of Cambria, there is no example of such a conspiracy as that infamous triumvirate now forms against me. Was it ever seen before that three great princes laid plot in concert to destroy a fourth, who had done nothing against them? I have not had the least quarrel either with France or with

Russia, still less with Sweden. If, in common life, three citizens took it into their heads to fall upon their neighbour and burn his house about him, they very certainly, by sentence of tribunal, would be broken on the wheel. What! and will sovereigns, who maintain these tribunals and these laws in their States, give such example to their subjects? Happy, my dear sister, is the obscure man whose good sense, from youth upwards, has renounced all sorts of glory; who, in his safe, low place, has none to envy him, and whose fortune does not excite the cupidity of scoundrels!

"But these reflections are vain! We have to be what our birth, which decides, has made us in entering upon this world. I reckoned that, being King, it beseemed me to think as a sovereign, and I took for principle that the reputation of a prince ought to be dearer to him than life. They have plotted against me; the Court of Vienna has given itself the liberty of trying to maltreat me; my honour commanded me not to suffer it. We have come to war; a gang of robbers falls on me, pistol in hand: that is the adventure which has happened to me. The remedy is difficult; in desperate diseases there are no methods but desperate ones.

"I beg a thousand pardons, dear sister; in these three long pages I talk to you of nothing but my troubles and affairs. A strange abuse it would be of any other person's friendship. But yours, my dear sister, yours is known to me; and I am persuaded you are not impatient when I open my heart to you—a heart which is yours altogether, being filled with sentiments of the tenderest esteem, with which I am, my dearest sister, yours, "F."

The first of Frederick's lamentation Psalms written during his reverses consists of an Epistle to Wilhelmina, and commences as follows :—

"O sweet and dear hope of my remaining days: O sister, whose friendship, so fertile in resources, shares all my sorrows, and with a helpful arm assists me in the gulf! It is in vain that the Destinies have overwhelmed me with disasters: if the crowd of Kings have sworn my ruin; if the earth have opened to swallow me—you still love me, noble and affectionate sister: loved by you, what is there of misfortune?"

In the terrible anxiety which this period brought upon the Margravine her conduct, no less indeed than at other times, revealed that while (as has been observed) she possessed the heart of a loving woman she had the head of a thoughtful man. Voltaire suggested to her that he might by means of influence with the French Court bring about a peace. She in reply wrote to him as follows :—

"*19th August*, 1757.

"One only knows one's friends when one is in trouble. The letter you have written to me does much honour to your manner of thinking. I do not know what way to testify to you how sensible I am of your conduct. The King is as much so as I am. You will find a note enclosed herewith which he has ordered me to send you. This great man is always the same. He bears his misfortunes with a courage and firmness worthy of him. He was not able to copy the letter he was writing to you. It began with some verses. Instead of throwing sand over it he took the inkstand, which is the reason that it is destroyed. I am in a terrible state, and will not survive the destruction of my house and my family. That is the only solution that is left to me. You will have some fine subjects for Tragedies. Oh! Times! Oh! Morals! You will perhaps draw tears by illusory reputation, whilst they contemplate with dry eyes the misfortunes of a whole house, against whom at bottom there is no real complaint. I cannot say more to you on this subject; my heart is so troubled that I know not what I am doing. But whatever may happen be assured that I am more than ever your Friend.

"WILHELMINA."

A further letter from Voltaire produced a reply from which the following is an extract:—

"*12th September*, 1757.

"Your letter has greatly touched me, and the one you addressed to the King has produced the same effect on him. I hope that you will be satisfied with his answer, as far as it concerns yourself; but you will be as little so as I am with his resolutions. I had flattered myself that your reflections would have made some impression on his mind. You will see the reverse in the enclosed note. It only remains to me to follow his destiny, if it is unfortunate. I have never prided myself on being a philosopher. I have tried to become one. The little progress I have made has taught me to despise greatness and riches; but I have found nothing in philosophy that is able to heal the wounds of the heart, except the means of getting rid of evils by ceasing to live. The state in which I am is worse than death. I see the greatest man of this century, my brother, my friend, reduced to the most fearful extremity. I see my entire family exposed to dangers and perils, my Fatherland torn by pitiless enemies, the country in which I am perhaps menaced by the same misfortunes. Would to God that I alone had to bear all the troubles I have just described to you; I would endure them with fortitude.

"WILHELMINA."

This letter as well as the following reveal something of the great straits in which

Frederick found himself. So great were the extremities to which he was reduced at this time that he had fully resolved on suicide rather than fall into the hands of his enemies, and his heroic sister had resolved to share his fate. The expostulations of Voltaire seem to have been in vain. Frederick again writes to his sister:—

"*17th September*, 1757.

"MY DEAREST SISTER,—I have no other consolation than in your precious letters. May heaven reward so much virtue and such heroic sentiments! Since I wrote last to you my misfortunes have but gone on accumulating. It seems as though Destiny would discharge all its wrath and fury upon the poor country which I had to rule over. The Swedes have entered Pommern. The French, after having concluded a Neutrality, humiliating to the King of England and themselves, are in full march upon Halberstadt and Magdeburg. From Prussen I am in daily expectation of hearing of a battle having been fought; the proportion of combatants being 25,000 against 80,000. The Austrians have marched into Silesia, whither the Prince of

Bevern follows them. I have advanced this way to fall upon the corps of the allied Army, which has run off and entrenched itself, behind Eisenach, amongst the hills, whither to follow, still more to attack them, all rules of war forbid. The moment I retire towards Saxony, this whole swarm will be upon my heels. Happen what may, I am determined, at all risks, to fall upon whatever corps of the enemy approaches mo nearest. I shall even bless Heaven for its mercy, if it grant me the favour to die sword in hand.

"Should this hope fail me, you will allow that it would be too hard to crawl at the feet of a company of traitors, to whom successful crimes have given the advantage to prescribe the law to me. How, my dear, my incomparable sister—how could I repress feelings of vengeance and of resentment against all my neighbours, of whom there is not one who did not accelerate my downfall, and will not share in our spoils? How could a Prince survive his State, the glory of his country, his own reputation? The Bavarian Elector, in his nonage, or, rather, in a sort of subjection to his Ministers, and dull to the biddings of honour, may give himself up as a slave to the imperious domination of the House of Austria, and kiss the hand which oppresses his father: I pardon it to his youth and his ineptitude. But is that the example for me to follow? No, dear sister; you think too nobly to give me such green advice. Is liberty—that precious prerogative—to be less dear to the sovereign in the eighteenth century than it was to Roman patricians of old? And where is it said that Brutus and Cato should carry magnanimity farther than princes and kings? Firmness consists in resisting misfortune; but only cowards submit to the yoke, bear patiently their chains, and support oppression tranquilly. Never, my dear sister, could I resolve upon such ignominy.

"If I had followed only my own inclinations I should have ended it at once, after that unfortunate battle which I lost. But I felt that this would be weakness, and that it behoved me to repair the evil which had happened. My attachment to the State awoke; I said to myself, it is not in seasons of prosperity that it is rare to find defenders, but in adversity. I made it a point of honour with myself to redress all that had got out of square, in which I was not unsuccessful, not even in the Lansitz (after those Zittau deserters) last of all. But no sooner do I hasten this way to face new enemies than Winterfield was beaten and killed near Gorlitz, than the French entered the heart of my States, than the Swedes blockaded Stettin. Now there is nothing effective left for me to do; there are too many enemies. Were I even to succeed in beating two armies, the third would crush me. The enclosed note will show you what I am still about to try; it is the last attempt.

"The gratitude, the tender affection which I feel towards you, that friendship, true as the hills, constrains me to deal openly with you. No, my divine sister, I shall conceal nothing from you that I intend to do; all my thoughts, all my resolutions shall be open and known to you in time. I will precipitate nothing; but also it will be impossible for me to change my sentiments.

"As for you, my incomparable sister, I have not the heart to turn you from your resolves. We think alike, and I cannot condemn in you the sentiments which I daily entertain. Life has been given to us as a benefit; when it ceases to be such . . . . I have nobody left in this world to attach me to it but you. My friends, the relations I loved most, are in the grave; in short, I have lost everything. If you take the resolution which I have taken, we end together our misfortunes and our unhappiness; and it will be the turn of them who remain in this world to provide for the concerns falling to their charge, and to bear the weight which has lain on us so long. These, my adorable sister, are sad reflections, but suitable to my present condition.

"But it is time to end this long, dreary letter, which treats almost of nothing but my own affairs. I have had some leisure, and have used it to open on you a heart filled with admiration and gratitude towards you. Yes, my adorable sister, if Providence troubled itself about human affairs, you ought to be the happiest person in the Universe. Your not being such confirms me in the sentiments expressed in the end of my *epitre*. In conclusion, believe that I adore you, and that I would give my life a thousand times to serve you. These are the sentiments which will animate me to the last breath of my life; being, my beloved sister, ever your "F."

Wilhelmina also writes:—

"*Baireuth, 15th September*, 1757.

"MY DEAREST BROTHER,—Your letter and the one you wrote to Voltaire, my dear brother, have almost killed me. What fatal resolutions, great God! Ah, my dear brother, you say you love me; and you drive a dagger into my heart. Your *epitre*, which I did receive, made me shed rivers of tears. I am now ashamed of such weakness. My misfortune would be so great that I should find worthier resources than tears. Your lot shall be mine. I will not survive either your misfortunes or those of the house I belong to. You may calculate that such is my firm resolution. But, after this avowal, allow me to entreat you to look back on what was the pitiable state of your enemy when you lay before Prag! It is the sudden whirl of Fortune for both parties. The like may occur again, when one is least expecting it. Cæsar was the slave of pirates, and he became the master of the world. A great genius like yourself finds resources even when all is lost; and it is impossible this phrenzy can continue. My heart bleeds to think of the poor souls in Preussen. What horrid barbarity, the detail of cruelties that go on there! I feel all that you feel on it, my dear brother. I know your heart, and your sensibility for your subjects.

"I suffer a thousand times more than I can tell you; nevertheless, hope does not abandon me. I received your letter of the 14th by W——. What kindness to think of me, who have nothing to give but a useless affection, which is so richly repaid by yours! I am obliged to finish; but I shall never cease to be, with the most profound respect [*tres profond* respect—that, and something still better, if my poor pen were not embarassed]—your "WILHELMINA."

On other discomforting rumours coming to the ears of the Margravine she writes:—

"*Baireuth*, 15*th October*, 1757.

"MY DEAR BROTHER,—Death and a thousand torments could not equal the frightful state I am in. There run reports that make me shudder. Some say you are wounded; others, dangerously ill. In vain have I tormented myself to have news of you; I can get none. Oh, my dear brother, come what may, I will not survive you. If I am to continue in this frightful uncertainty, I cannot stand it; I shall sink under it, and then I shall be happy. I have been on the point of sending you a courier; but (environed as we are) I durst not. In the name of God bid somebody write me one word.

"I know not what I have written; my heart is torn in pieces; I feel that by dint of disquietude and alarms I am losing my wits. Oh, my dear adorable brother, have pity on me! Heaven grant I be mistaken, and that you may scold me; but the least thing that concerns you pierces me to the heart, and alarms my affection too much. Might I die a thousand times, provided you lived and were happy!

"I can say no more. Grief chokes me; and I can only repeat that your fate shall be mine; being, my dear brother, your

"WILHELMINA."

The day following she writes to Voltaire :—

"16th October, 1757.

"Overwhelmed by sufferings of mind and body, I am able only to write a little letter. You will find one enclosed herewith which will reward you a hundred-fold for my brevity. Our situation is always the same. A grave is the extent of our view. Although everything seems lost, things remain to us which cannot be taken away; they are fortitude and the sentiments of the heart. Be persuaded of our gratitude, and of all the sentiments which you deserve by your attachment and way of thinking, worthy of a true philosopher.

"WILHELMINA."

The following letter from Frederick crossed the previous one from his sister:—

"*Eilenburg*, 17th October, 1757.

"MY DEAREST SISTER,—What is the good of philosophy unless we employ it in the disagreeable moments of life? It is then, my dear sister, that courage and firmness avail us.

"I am now in motion; and having once got into that, you may calculate I shall not think of sitting down again, except under improved omens. If outrage irritates even cowards, what will it do to hearts that have courage?

"I foresee I shall not be able to write again for perhaps six weeks; which fails not to be a sorrow to me; but I entreat you to be calm during these turbulent affairs, and to wait with patience the month of December; paying no regard to the Nurnberg newspapers, nor to those of the Reich, which are totally Austrian.

"I am as tired as a dog. I embrace you with my whole heart; being with the most perfect affection, my dearest sister, your

"FREDERICK."

Having had a success, he writes (November 5, 1757) to inform her of it, and concludes:—"You, my dear sister, my good, my divine and affectionate sister, who deign to interest yourself in the fate of a brother who adores you, deign also to share in my joy. The instant I have time I will tell you more. I embrace you with my whole heart. Adieu!

"F."

The last year of her life closed very gloomily for the Margravine. Notwithstanding some successes the chances were fearfully against her brother, and his reverses were great. She ardently longed for peace, as well for the sake of the country as for that of her brother, and she would willingly have sacrificed her life for it. Writing to Voltaire on 2nd January, 1758, she says: "Thank Heaven we have finished the most fatal of years. You say so many kind things in reference to the present one, that they form one reason the more for my gratitude. I wish you everything that can make you perfectly happy. As regards myself, I leave my fate to destiny. We often form desires which would be very prejudicial if accomplished, therefore I form no more. If anything in the world could satisfy my desires, it would be peace; I think as you do about war, and we have quite a third who certainly thinks as we do. But can we always act up to what we think? Is it not necessary to submit to many prejudices established since the world began?"

As the year advanced the health of the Margravine visibly declined. Whilst her enfeebled frame was at Baireuth her heart was with her brother, bleeding at every fresh reverse. Frederick in a letter to his brother, alluding to her prostrate condition, says: "What you write to me of my sister of Baireuth makes me tremble! Next to our Mother, she is what I have the most tenderly loved in this world. She is a sister who has my heart and all my confidence; and whose character is of price beyond all the crowns in this universe. From my tenderest years, I was brought up with her; you can conceive how there reigns between us that indissoluble bond of mutual affection and attachment for life, which, in all other cases, were it only for disparity of ages, is impossible. Would to Heaven I might die before her—and that this terror itself don't take away my life without my actually losing her."

The Margravine's last letter was, we are told, written on the 18th July, 1758, with trembling hand " almost illegible." Replying, the King says: "O you, the dearest of my family, you, whom I have most at heart of all in this world—for the sake of whatever is most precious to you, preserve yourself; and let me have at least the consolation of shedding my tears in your bosom!"

The last letter from Voltaire to the Margravine is dated the 27th September, 1758, in which he urges her to consult the celebrated physician Tronchin. But the suggestion was too late or of no avail. "Wilhelmina, who had ever been so ready with her pen, was no longer able to use it, not even to bid a last farewell to her friend. Yet, in token of how much her thoughts were with him, she sent him her picture a fortnight before her end, as a last message of friendship and gratitude. Soon her spirit would fathom the great mysteries which had occupied her during her life. Who is there who would not believe in affection's double sight? In the same night, at the same hour in which her brother suffered a crushing defeat at the hands of the Austrians at Hochkirch, Wilhelmina breathed her last, on the 14th October, 1758. Her last words, her last thoughts were for the happiness and welfare of the King. She desired to have her brother's letters buried with her. This wish was, however, not fulfilled. At her especial request the funeral oration to be held at her grave was to contain but little mention of herself, the vanity of all human things being made the chief subject of it. She was buried according to her instructions, in the simplest and quietest manner, in the chapel of the Castle of Baireuth."*

The King's sorrow, on receiving the intelligence of his sister's death, was uncontrollable. The friend, the confidant, the consolation of his life was gone in his darkest hour, when he seemed to have the most need of her sound advice and sustaining comfort. "How," says he, "can I make up for the loss which everything warns me of; how can I replace this beloved and adorable sister, who has loved me so dearly? How could I believe that she, to whom, since my earliest youth, I have confided my every thought, should so soon be taken from me?" He made a pathetic appeal to Voltaire to write something in her memory, and, not being satisfied with one effort, he writes:—"For what I have asked of you, I assure you I have very much at heart; be it prose, be it verse, it is all the same to me. A monument is necessary to commemorate that virtue so pure, so rare, which has not been

* "The Margravine of Baireuth and Voltaire." By H.R.H. Princess Christian, p. 126.

sufficiently generally known. If I was persuaded I could write adequately myself, I would charge no one with it; but as you are certainly the first of our age, I can address myself only to you."

In response to this appeal, Voltaire wrote the following ode:—

Ombre illustre, ombre chère; âme héroïque et pure;
Toi que mes tristes yeux ne cessent de pleurer,
Quand la fatale loi de toute la nature
    Te conduit dans la sepulture,
    Faut-il te plaindre ou t'admirer ?

Les vertus, les talents ont été ton partage ;
  Tu vécus, tu mourus en sage ;
Et, voyant à pas lents avancer le trépas,
    Tu montras le même courage,
  Qui fait voler ton frère au milieu des combats.

Femme sans préjuges, sans vice et sans molless
  Tu bannis loin de toi la superstition,
  Fille de l'imposture et de l'ambition
Qui tyrannise la faiblesse.

Les langueurs, les tourments, ministres de la mo
  T'avaient déclaré la guerre ;
Tu les bravas sans effort,
  Tu plaignis ceux de la terre.

Hélas ! si tes conseils avaient pu l'emporter
  Sur le faux interêt d'une aveugle vengeance
Que de torrents de sang on eut vus s'arrêter
    Quel bonheur, t'aurait dû la France.

Ton cher frère aujourd'hui, dans un noble repos,
Recueillerait son âme, à soi-même rendue;
Le philosophe, le héros,
Ne serait affligé que de t'avoir perdue.

Sur ta cendre adorée, il jetterait des fleurs
 Du haut de son char de victoire;
 Et les mains de la paix, et les mains de la gloire
Se joindraient pour sècher ses pleurs.

Sa voix célèbrerait ton amitie fidèle,
 Les échos de Berlin répondraient à ses chants;
 Ah ! j'impose silence à mes tristes accents,
Ils n'appartient qu'à lui de te rendre immortelle.

While Wilhelmina's devotion to her brother was absorbing and self-sacrificing, her friendship to Voltaire was constant and faithful. And may we not hope that he felt the benefit of a contact with her more than even appears? One of her letters to him contains in a few words a statement of the simple Christian faith that was hers:—"I pity," she says, "your blindness only to believe in one God and to deny Jesus."

Frederick had erected in his garden at Sans-Souci a temple in memory of his sister dedicated to "Friendship." Although his life was darkened by her loss, his subsequent victories and final conquest, and the peaceful evening of his life, justified the belief she always had in his greatness and ultimate success.

The Margravine had one child only, the Princess Elizabeth Frederike Sophie, who afterwards became Duchess of Wurtemburg. Writing of her, Voltaire says that she was the most beautiful child in Europe, that he should have recognised her without warning, that she had the turn of her mother's face with Frederick's eyes. As this lady died childless the Margravine lives only "in minds made better" by her life; but we cannot doubt that in many ways her influence still lives, and that the intellectual life of Germany owes much to her bright and stimulating example.

SUSANNE KOSSUTH MESZLENYI.

SUSANNE KOSSUTH MESZLENYI.

However surely it may be the inevitable lot of small Nationalities to become merged in larger and neighbouring Empires, we cannot but sympathise with their yearnings for independence. We instinctively admire the patriotic devotion of their noblest sons, who, at the call of duty, or what they believe to be such, arise as avengers of their country's wrongs, too frequently only to die in her service.

The history of Hungary is tragic, and her lot is sad. As an Austrian dependency Hungary has from time to time possessed a powerful internal government, only to have her growing liberties curtailed and her aspirations crushed, and the proceedings of her Senate disregarded by despotic sovereigns.

No small portion of her troubles have arisen from the fact of her being peopled by distinct races. After the stirring times of 1847 and the early part of 1848, the position of Hungary seemed better than it had been for centuries. Their just claims had been tardily recognised, liberty of the Press and annual Diets conceded. It was then in the first instance the act of their countrymen, the Croatians, that led to the sanguinary quarrels afterwards adopted by Austria and joined by Russia, which resulted so disastrously to the Magyar race.

In these sanguinary struggles Louis Kossuth, the eloquent and enthusiastic patriot, occupied a commanding position. His distinguished services not only in the Senate, but also on the field of battle, were so greatly aided and stimulated by his helpful and devoted sister Susanne, that a brief notice of her in these pages cannot be out of place.

Hers is not an example of early influence, for Susanne Kossuth, the youngest member of the family, was born in the year 1820, at a time when her brother, the future patriot, was already verging upon manhood.

In her earlier years she received a careful training at the hands of a private tutor, the prevalent custom among the higher class of Hungarians. The education given to girls in that country is, or was, one friendly to the development of an intellectual and thoughtful character—music, drawing, the art of composition, modern languages, and literature forming essential parts. History, also, so stimulating to a thoughtful patriotism, is especially cultivated. The girls are also early trained in habits of industry, and, even in the highest circles, to become capable household managers.

The knowledge of history acquired by Susanne not only drew out and disciplined her young intellect, but roused in her that love of country which was so characteristic in her family, and which was such a dominant power in her own life. " The private tutors in Hungary are men of high standing, not only socially and morally, but intellectually; cherished guests and friends of the families in which they reside, who consort with the parents in a frank and noble way, and hence the high character and tone of education among their women."

The parents of Susanne removed to Pesth whilst she was young, which had the effect of somewhat shortening her scholastic training. But her best education did not, therefore, cease. Her father, who, assisted by her brother, conducted the *Pesth Hirlap*, having a rheumatic affection of the hand, Susanne acted as his amanuensis, and became his fellow-labourer and active helper. And when the printing of the *Hirlap* was suppressed, she herself took a considerable share in the tedious task of copying it. It was not conducted on the ordinary lines of a newspaper, either political or business, but was patriotic in its character and aim. "Its object was to develop the national constitution, by peaceable reform and construction, from within outward." It has been said: "From the fifty-two countries into which Hungary was divided were regularly received letters upon every national interest—material, social, and intellectual. It was the part of the younger Kossuth to answer these by leading articles, elaborating principles, while his father and sister would make a digest, and put into form the correspondence itself. Such labours were a fitting occupation for her honest and magnanimous soul, and a providential preparation for the duties of the last years of her life."

When Susanne was about twenty years of age she married Rudolf Meszlenyi, an untitled gentleman whose sister had married Louis Kossuth. He was possessed of an estate which afforded a sufficient income. The marriage appears—so far at any rate as regards its highest purposes, a true union of heart and life—to have been a singularly happy one. We have lately read of a distinguished English lady who, on receiving a proposal of marriage after her own heart, knelt down on the green turf and thanked God for the happiness brought into her life. Susanne Meszlenyi, in speaking during her sad and lonely widowhood of the high character of her husband, used to tell how she loved, in after years, to go to pray in the chapel at Buda in which she was married, and would kiss the very stones on which she stood at the altar.

Madame Meszlenyi shared her husband's hopes and aspirations—rather, they were her own. Her married life was, however, destined to be of short duration. Two little daughters and a son were added to the number of her loved ones ; but a short time afterwards, in the early part of 1847, her husband sacrificed his life through an act of patriotic devotion. As a member of County Sessions, a question of great interest, and thought by Meszlenyi to be one of great importance affecting certain judiciary privileges, having arisen, he, desiring to secure the interest of another member, at the last moment, rode day and night for the purpose of seeing and influencing him. Congestion of the brain and delirium followed upon the self-forgetful exertion. Madame Meszlenyi being at the time herself very ill at home, her husband not wishing to expose her to the fatigues of a long journey, managed to send daily despatches in the hope of hiding from her his serious condition. But, as is so frequently the case, the eye of love read between the lines, and the heart of love divined the distant trouble. Madame Meszlenyi went to her husband, only arriving in time to see him die.

It was about this time—March, 1847—that, chiefly in return for the services of Louis Kossuth in connection with the rescue of certain members of the Imperial family during recent revolutionary troubles at Vienna, certain valuable constitutional rights were allowed to Hungary. These concessions went very far towards satisfying the national yearning, and were the occasion of great rejoicing. This following so closely after the sad bereavement of Madame Meszlenyi again made her ill, prostrating her with violent spasms of neuralgia. This has been mentioned as showing her highly strung nervous temperament and "exquisite sensibility."

But war came to this unhappy country all too swiftly in the wake of the much-prized privileges. The claims of Hungary had no sooner been acknowledged than it would seem that the Austrian Court repented their magnanimity, and, by holding out certain hopes to the Croatians, induced them to commence hostilities against the Magyars, who constituted the principal part of the Hungarian nationalty.

Kossuth, as a foremost member of the Hungarian Diet, took a prominent part in the preparations for the campaign. In one important respect he knew where to look for sympathy and help. He has spoken of his sister Susanne as his twin soul. "He knew," it is said, "of what extraordinary action she was capable. His conviction that her health and strength, like his own, being mainly spiritual in its source, would come at the call of the patriot's hope and humanity's cause, was justified by all he knew of her antecedent life, and all we know of her subsequent action. It was not the great work of a great sphere that was unhealthy for her. She could sink only when she was not allowed scope for her soul's expansion, or when means failed her to carry out her plans."

It was no small thing for Kossuth to be able to say to her, " Upon you I must depend to see to the wounded. Proceed in your own way, and call for means as you need them."

Finding herein work for her womanly heart and active mind, she rose above her sorrow in her country's need. She began her task by inserting in the organ of the new Government an eloquent and passionate appeal for the help of her countrywomen, in alleviating the wounded, by combining their efforts and forming small societies and temporary hospitals throughout the country. The call from the sister of the patriot to whom all eyes were turned was not in vain, but met with a general response. Madame Meszlenyi herself took journeys throughout the country, "organising, arranging, watching for everything, keeping all accounts, making all disbursements." In this way she had under management in different parts of the country no less than seventy-two hospitals. So great was the enthusiasm which her brother's name and her country's call aroused, that during her journeys she frequently came to places from which all the able-bodied men had gone to the war.

It is stated that on one occasion at Erlau Madame Meszlenyi found it necessary to apply for the use of a monastery for the purposes of a hospital. She went to the Superior and urged her request. In answer she was informed that the monastery was full. She thereupon urged that the inmates should crowd, so as to make room for the accommodation of the wounded. On the Superior still objecting to having the monastery turned into a hospital, Madame Meszlenyi desired to be allowed to see the rooms and suggested how the needful alterations could be made. At length her earnestness and energy prevailed with the lethargic ecclesiastics, the Superior not only consenting that everything should be done as she wished, but at once set about doing it. When the wounded were brought she did not allow her love of her countrymen to quench her humanity, but cared for Magyar and Croatian and Austrian alike, showing, however,. her inborn delicacy and thoughtfulness in directing that they should be put into different rooms. Such was her careful attention to the needs and wishes of the poor sufferers that they said they were enveloped by the atmosphere of a mother's tenderness.

Nor were her qualifications for the skilled nursing of wounded soldiers less than those which distinguished her as an administrator. Her moral influence was great. The enthusiastic eloquence of her conversation with the sufferers, as they could endure it, went far to rob the pillow of its weariness and the wound of its pain. " She understood the importance of ministering to the imagination and heart when the excitements of the battlefield were exchanged for the bed of suffering."

The enthusiastic and grateful people strove in many ways to show their appreciation of the unselfish devotion of Madame Meszlenyi. It is recorded that during one of her journeys, having one night reached a village from which all the men had gone to the war, and being at the inn for the night, she was surprised by hearing music, whereupon she went to the window, and was astonished at seeing the village girls, dressed in white, carrying a rustic banner and baskets of flowers. Having heard of her presence in the village, they had come in procession to the house where she was staying to express in the best way they could their gratitude for the loving devotion shown by the sister of Kossuth towards their brothers and fathers in the war. Madame Meszlenyi kindly received her young admirers, and was much affected by the sense of their love. She accepted the little token of their gratitude, but took care to impress upon them strongly that she wished for no thanks; that she was doing no more than they themselves; that it was actual pain for her to receive any marks of personal honours in the time of their country's peril and need, when self should be lost sight of. This desire to sink and forget herself and her achievements for the sake of the principles which governed her actions was characteristic of her throughout. Sympathy in the cause for which she laboured, in the motives which animated her, she welcomed, whilst she invariably shrank from praise for individual exertion.

Although brilliant successes attended the efforts of the Magyars, who might have subdued the insurgent tribes, and even held their own against the Austrians, it might have been apparent that the struggle was hopeless when the aid of Russia was obtained, and Hungary invaded from all quarters. But no one appears to have been prepared for the surrender of the Hungarian General to the Russian forces at Grosswardein. Upon this Kossuth and some of his immediate friends found refuge in Turkey which honourably refused to give them up, and from where they subsequently made their way to England, and eventually to the New World.

Madame Meszlenyi was not so fortunate in misfortune as her brother. She had followed the army in the hope of joining her brother, and had on this journey the additional misfortune of losing her only son. She and the other members of her family, including the aged mother, and the ten children of herself and sister, fifteen in all, were arrested at Grosswardein. Notwithstanding her mother's illness, they were all for a time kept confined in one room. The Russian Commander on being appealed to proved more humane than the Austrian. Madame Meszlenyi eloquently urged that, being prisoners of war, and that a war for their country, they ought not to be treated as criminals; and the officer placed at her disposal a deserted house. Although the place was carefully guarded, they were for the period of two months (during which the Russians occupied Grosswardein) protected from all danger and insult. Upon the withdrawal of the Russians, the General informed Madame Meszlenyi that although he would do what he could on her behalf he could not undertake to tell what course might be adopted. And no sooner had the Russian forces withdrawn than they were informed that they must immediately prepare to be taken to Pesth. Notwithstanding the fact that Madame Meszlenyi informed the officer that one of her children was suffering from scarlet fever and would die if removed, which was corroborated by the doctor who was in attendance upon her, her plea was of no avail. They were compelled to go. Madame Meszlenyi afterwards said: "God saw that I could not have borne to lose her." And her child did not die.

At Pesth they were subject to much privation. Their prison quarters were comfortless, destitute of furniture, with only straw for the invalids, and open to the gaze of the soldiery. This continued for many months. When, at last, Madame Meszlenyi was brought to trial she pleaded her own cause, maintaining "that she had done only what womanly duty and Hungarian right imposed on her conscience and sense of honour." So eloquently did she plead for her own and her children's liberty, and exhibit such a wide knowledge of the constitution of the country, and a power of grasping every detail, and meeting every difficulty of the position, that the judge before whom she was tried said, in astonishment: "What shall I do with this woman?" The principal ground of Madame Meszlenyi's skilfully-argued defence was that she had nothing to do with the war, which was entirely the result of the deliberations and actions of those who had the conduct of state matters, but her own conduct had been in the service of humanity only, that she had not been engaged in making war, but only in succouring the wounded in war. But the eloquent pleading of Madame Meszlenyi was in vain; and had not help come from an unexpected quarter, her heroic soul would have flashed out from the scaffold. At the last moment, however, officers of the Austrian army petitioned the Court and urged in her favour her humane action towards the wounded of their own army. "We," they said, "and multitudes of Austrians owe our lives to the magnanimity of this woman." And this truthful plea prevailed. She had seen only fellow creatures in suffering, and directing all the wounded on the field to be brought to her hospitals, she had tenderly nursed and cared for friend and enemy alike. "The poor fellows are often on our side in their hearts," she would say. The result of this disinterested interposition on her behalf was that, instead of the prisoner being condemned to the scaffold, she was, for the time being, honourably acquitted.

After her release Madame Meszleyni continued to reside in Pesth with her mother. The confiscation of her property rendered it necessary that she should have recourse to some means of livelihood, although, had she been willing to live on bounty, the sister of Kossuth would have known no want. She consequently engaged in the, to her, congenial task of the education of the young; and so thorough and conscientious and loving was the manner of her work in this, as in everything to which she put her hand, that success began to crown her endeavours. Her movements were, however, strictly under the eye of the Austrian Government, who became afraid that her school might be the means of promulgating the obnoxious principles of patriotism. It was accordingly required of her that she would undertake that she would not teach history. Her answer was that she could not give an undertaking contrary to her principles, and the school had accordingly to be abandoned.

Her freedom itself proved to be only of short duration. Notwithstanding every caution and endeavour to keep herself aloof from anything of a public character, Madame Meszlenyi was rudely aroused on a stormy midnight in December, 1851, and hurried away by Austrian soldiers, being compelled to leave the terrified and afflicted members of her family. In response to her urgent inquiries as to the fate of her mother and children no information could she gain, except that they were also under arrest. This delicate lady was once again cast into a common prison, where she was attended only by soldiers, and suffered such privation from exposure and cold that she became seriously ill, and was seized with a protracted fever, the effects of which, and of an affection of the lungs, then contracted, never left her.

The aged mother had also meanwhile been placed under arrest, but, having her grandchildren about her, the scene of confusion which arose rendered her insensible. Her daughter Emilie having been arrested and brought by another company of soldiers, and seeing her mother apparently lifeless on the ground, broke from her guard, and kneeling beside her mother begged for medical aid to be summoned to her. The sickness which followed also in the case of Madame Kossuth rendered it impracticable for her to be removed, and she was accordingly allowed to remain in the house with Emilie and the grandchildren, though all remained under strict guard.

Madame Meszlenyi herself was kept in confinement on this occasion for a period of five months, day and night exposed to the eyes of the guard. What she suffered during this period none may know. Rigorous means were taken to prevent any communication with the outer world.

At length proposals were made by the Austrian Government that they should all be set at liberty on condition that they should forthwith leave the Continent, proceeding in secrecy and disguise. Had the determination of Madame Meszlenyi affected herself alone she would have refused to accept freedom on such terms, but for the sake of her children, as well as that of her sister, she determined to accept the terms of banishment from her native country, which she loved so well, and for which she had suffered so much. Without having the opportunity of bidding farewell to many whom they loved, the exiled party proceeded as far as Brussels, where they were obliged to wait in consequence of the condition of Madame Kossuth. Meanwhile, on it becoming known that the mother and sisters of Kossuth intended to proceed to America, it was suggested to Kossuth (who was then in New York) that he should deliver a lecture to raise funds on their behalf. This resulted in about 1,000 dollars.

Emilie and part of her family only, however, proceeded forthwith, Madame Meszlenyi and Madame Rutkai, with their children, remaining behind at the risk of being given up to the Austrian Government.

While in Brussels, in writing to a friend in England she concludes as follows: "I can write but little and seldom; of our country I cannot; of foreign affairs I shall not; of myself—what could I write of my own self? My head and my spirits have grown grey! My heart is become old, decrepit, and age is sterile! You must not make any mention of even these short epistles.

"My sick mother, Louise, and myself will stay here. Emily will in a short time leave for America with her whole family. My children have grown in these adverse circumstances, with less favourable developments than I once expected. The loss may, however, be still recovered; there is as yet time for it. They, too, send you their love. How could you have supposed of me that I could have loved my children to forget my friend? You say you are not changed. God be praised for it! I, too, can say that I am not changed in anything—no not even in respect to my faith in mankind. I have a strong will, in spite of so many bitter disappointments. And so I address you in the open-hearted voice of old friendship, and I expect your letters written in the same spirit. Let me not wait long for them. God bless you, and may He extend over your life all the good which is contained in the best wishes of your dear friend,

"MESZLENYI."

During her enforced stay at Brussels Madame Meszlenyi sought amongst the lace manufacturers to obtain work as a means of support of herself and those dependent upon her. She set about learning to make the lace, and, having learnt, worked with such constant industry that she was not only able to maintain the family, but at the end of about eighteen months, when her mother died. she had saved a small sum of money, which she invested in lace to be used when she arrived in the New World.

With the death of her mother the necessity for any longer stay in Brussels came to an end. Madame Meszlenyi, and her sister, Madame Ruttkai, accordingly proceeded to the land of their exile.

Arriving at New York, Madame Meszlenyi found it necessary at once to take steps for the maintenance of the party. Her reply to an enquiry whether anything could be done for her was, " Give me work." And in her endeavours she was as fertile as in her labours she was indefatigable. She not only started a store for the sale of lace, which she superintended and took a place at the desk, but finding further exertion necessary, added to her business that of dressmaking, which she had also, with a thoughtful eye to the future of the children, learnt at Brussels.

But while carrying on business in the manner in which her sense of duty required it, Madame Meszleyni's days were numbered. Never strong, the trials and exposure of the night of her last arrest had effected their work of ravage in her constitution. Had she been able to have succeeded the leisure and refreshment of the sea voyage] by rest and care, the course of disease might have been arrested and her life spared for many years. But she felt that necessity was laid upon her for work, for immediate and constant work. And having undertaken any duty, she would perform it at whatever cost to herself. The requirements of her dressmaking business would often, in the absence of sufficient help, find this heroic and high-born lady burning the midnight oil, to herself finish a dress which had been promised by a certain time.

The knowledge of her condition no doubt stimulated her exertion. She knew that her days were numbered; and she had an object to accomplish. She wished to leave behind her sufficient means to provide a good education for her little girls, so that they might thus be put into the way of earning their own livelihood as teachers. And although it was often represented to Madame Meszlenyi that in the event of her dying her children would be taken care of, the independence of her spirit would flash into her face while she declared that she only desired that her children should have the opportunity of working as she had done herself.

As may, however, be imagined, the difficulties and trials of these Hungarian women were many. But, notwithstanding all discouragements, the growing feebleness of the moving spirit of all, the spark of life burning but dimly, the well-being of her children kept the flickering flame alive. But the finely-strung spirit was strained to the utmost. Friends were not wanting; but, like many another whose soul has been touched to its finest issues, Madame Meszlenyi could not endure the thought of either herself or her children being dependent on charity. Upon her physician saying that she must have rest and change apart from the scene of her labours, a lady, who had been her friend from the first, offered her an old family mansion. Other friends came to her with offers of money, and provided a fund for a period of rest. It went much against her inclination to accept help so willingly offered. She said with a flood of tears: " We did not come to this country counting upon sympathy, but to work, as we heard everybody here could do. Heretofore in no distressing circumstances have I lost my courage, nor have I lost it now. But this illness is the hand of God; to Him I now yield in accepting charity."

Madame Meszlenyi endeavoured vainly to recruit her strength sufficiently to enable her to make a voyage to Belgium in order to engage lace workers, and to found a permanent and prosperous business, in which she might before her own death obtain a partner who might provide the means of accomplishing what lay so near her own heart, the completion of the education of her daughters when she should be taken from them.

As the winter of 1853 thus passed, and the succeeding spring opened, difficulties arose which had not been anticipated, while the exertion which was attendant upon explanations and negotiations was more than the feeble spirit was able to bear. Even after arrangements had been made for her voyage to Europe in the hope that success in her endeavours might stimulate her energies, and yet prolong her life, it became evident that nothing in this world could avail further—that if her earthly hopes were to be brought to fruition it would be by other hands than hers.

It is some satisfaction for us to know that when Madame Meszlenyi learnt at last that it would be impossible for her to accomplish the desire of her heart, the friend in whose house she had resided during the winter cheered her by an assurance that her children would be provided for, and that the education so wisely begun under the eye of the mother would be completed according to her desire. As this desire was fully known to her beloved sister Emilie, this assurance proved to be a great consolation to the dying mother.

The last scene should be told in the words of one who speaks with authority.

"In the course of June she called for the administration of the Lord's Supper, which she took for the last time from the hands of the Lutheran clergyman, and continually afterwards expressed that she was ready and anxious to go. On the afternoon of the 28th of that month she said to those around her that the hour was approaching, and summoned her sister Ruttkai and the children to the leave-taking, at which was also present one of her family physicians, the sister of her heart and soul being far away.

"Having said the last tender words, and embraced them, she looked at the doctor earnestly, and inaudibly pronounced the words ' How long ? ' ' Not long,' he replied gently, and she brilliantly smiled. She breathed some hours after, but said nothing more except to give a negative when asked if she were in pain. A humble Hungarian friend who sat by her bedside, watching her last breath, and at last closed her eyes, has said that an hour before she died so brilliant a look came into her face she thought she was going to rally, and perhaps recover. She then attempted to give her a message to Emilie, of which she uttered not words enough to be wholly understood by the auditor; then the wonderful expression faded, and hardly had done so when the last breath came. It was on the 29th June, 1854, when this noble and gifted being, at the early age of thirty-four, ascended to the Father of Spirits."

The aged brother and patriot yet lives in the neighbourhood of Turin, where his last years are being spent in the society of his surviving sister, Madame Ruttkai.

CAROLINE LUCRETIA HERSCHEL.

CAROLINE LUCRETIA HERSCHEL.

> The heights by great men reached and kept
>   Were not attained by sudden flight;
> But they, while their companions slept,
>   Were toiling upward in the night.
>
> LONGFELLOW.

GEORGES SAND has somewhere said that the only virtue is the eternal sacrifice of self—a remark which will bear careful consideration. If we do well because it is pleasant to do so, or for a reward to be obtained, there does not seem to be much merit in so doing. But if, to our own sacrifice and discomfort, we follow the right for the sake only of duty, then, whether the motive be love to God or man, the thorny road will at last lead to the sunny tableland— to the home of content. The remark is commonplace; but it is the common that needs most to be remembered.

Among instances of self-abnegation we have

that of Caroline Herschel—brave, loving, and unwearying, following with unwavering devotion the path of patient duty until it became one of abounding pleasure. But it was not with thoughts of self; self-love moved not the tender heart, the strong will, the willing hand. Love of her brother set in motion the will of a whole-souled woman; and while she sought only to be his humble helper, she was destined to share in his greatness.

Caroline Lucretia Herschel was a member of a Hanoverian family, many of whom, if not born to greatness, signally achieved it. She was born in the month of March, 1750, having a sister many years older and several brothers, one of whom—William—became the famous astronomer. Her father—Isaac Herschel— was the master of a military band, and took delight in encouraging the cultivation of music in his children. In this as well as his devotion to his other studies, William displayed unusual talent and perseverance. It is stated that although his brother Jacob was four years older, William "mastered the French language in half the time needed by the elder."

In the large family of the Herschels the lot

of the little Caroline does not seem to have been over bright, or her education much cared for. They were, however, an intelligent household, the elder ones attaining considerable proficiency in music, William by no means limiting his desires in that direction. In her diary, in which Caroline afterwards noted reminiscences of her early days, she mentions the enlivening conversations on musical and philosophical subjects which frequently kept her father and brothers engaged until morning. "Often," she says, "I would keep myself awake that I might listen to their animating remarks, *for it made me so happy to see them so happy.*"

Caroline for some time attended with her brothers the garrison school; but her mother's ambition for her seems only to have been that she should learn domestic duties and needlework. This arose from no disregard on the part of the excellent mother as to her daughter's well-being, but from the idea that much book-learning was not desirable in girls. Her father, however, found opportunities for instructing his little daughter in music. He would himself have given her, according to her own desire, a superior education, had it not been for the opposition of her mother. So little Caroline was in danger of growing up a household drudge in a straitened home. But *L'homme propose, et Dieu dispose.* A visit to England of the regiment to which they were attached resulted in William settling in Bath as a musician. He had always been to Caroline the dear brother. While her inability to satisfy the dainty tastes of her "gentleman" brother Jacob had earned her many a whipping, the considerate love of William had come into her young life as a soothing balm, a stimulating power. And, like good seed, it brought forth fruit a hundredfold.

The loss of her father, when she was seventeen years old, was to Caroline a source of great sorrow. In him she lost the one whom, next to her now absent brother, she loved. With his death all hope of further education for Caroline came to an end, and for some years further her life as maid of all work continued.

A change, however, as unexpected as it was decisive, came into her life when she was about twenty-two years old. Her brother

William being over on a visit from England, suggested that she should return with him to Bath, which proved to be the opening of a new era.

Being settled at Bath Miss Herschel entered with ardour into her brother's career as musician and his studies as astronomer. He toiled hard in his profession for the purpose of gaining a livelihood, at the same time reading and working for the object nearest his heart. In both his pursuits his sister became his ready and laborious helper—his constant and sympathising companion. For this purpose she acquired a considerable proficiency in music, and for many years assisted her brother, not only by copying musical scores for large orchestras, but also in taking part in lessons and rehearsals, and herself singing in oratorios conducted by him.

The industry of both brother and sister at this period of their joint labours seems, indeed, to have been almost without parallel. While, their days were given to musical work to such an extent as would have sufficed for an ordinary occupation—and that a busy one—their nights were devoted to the heavens, and to the manufacture of telescopes and telescopic appliances on a scale hitherto unknown.

William Herschel's fame as an astronomer, inventor, and discoverer having become established, in 1782 he gave up his attention to music, in order to devote himself entirely to astronomical research, and was appointed Royal Astronomer. In this year he removed to Datchet, and, a few years after, to Slough. Absorbing as was their pursuit, it was carried on at an enormous self-sacrifice and hardship, and was not by any means free from danger. Miss Herschel writes in her diary : " That my fears of danger and accidents were not wholly imaginary I had an unlucky proof on the night of the 31st December. The evening had been cloudy, but about ten o'clock a few stars became visible, and in the greatest hurry all was got ready for observing. My brother, at the front of the telescope, directed me to make some alteration in the lateral motion, which was done by machinery, on which the point of support of the tube and mirror rested. At each end of the machine or trough was an iron hook, such as butchers use for hanging their joints upon, and having to run in the dark on ground covered a foot deep with melting snow, I fell on one of these hooks, which entered my right leg above the knee. My brother's call, 'Make haste!' I could only answer by a pitiful cry, 'I am hooked!' He and the workman were instantly with me, but they could not lift me without leaving nearly two ounces of my flesh behind. The workman's wife was called, but I was afraid to do anything, and I was obliged to be my own surgeon by applying aquabusade and tying a kerchief about it for some days, till Dr. Lind, hearing of my accident, brought me ointment and lint, and told me how to use them. At the end of six weeks I began to have some fears about my poor limb, and asked again for Dr. Lind's opinion. He said if a soldier had met with such a hurt, he would have been entitled to six weeks' nursing in a hospital. I had, however, the comfort to know that my brother was no loser through the accident, for the remainder of the night was cloudy, and several nights afterwards afforded only a few short intervals favourable for sweeping, and until the 16th of January there was no necessity for my exposing myself for a whole night to the severity of the season."

"It would be impossible for me," she also writes, "if it were required, to give a regular account of all that passed around me in the lapse of the two following years, for they were spent in a perfect chaos of business. The garden and workrooms were swarming with labourers and workmen, smiths and carpenters going to and fro between the forge and the forty-foot machinery, and I ought not to forget that there is not one screw-bolt about the whole apparatus but what was fixed under the immediate eye of my brother. I have seen him lie stretched many an hour, in a burning sun, across the top beam whilst the iron-work for the various motions was being fixed. At one time no less than twenty-four men (twelve and twelve relieving each other) kept polishing day and night; my brother, of course, never leaving them all the while, taking his food without allowing himself time to sit down to table."

Miss Herschel's services to her brother, as well as to science as an independent discoverer, were recognised, when, in 1787, she was appointed assistant to her brother at a salary of £50 per annum.

In the following year, after she had enjoyed the closest companionship and identity with her brother for sixteen years, Mr. Herschel's marriage brought a considerable change in the life of the sister. Her devotion to his interests and pursuits became no less, but the supreme place by his side was gone.

Although Miss Herschel seems to have felt keenly the separation from her brother in domestic life, her zeal in the objects to which he had devoted himself never waned. Having entered upon them from a sense of grateful love, she became passionately attached to the work. Although living apart from him, she continued to the end of his life to be his indefatigable assistant, as well as an independent observer of the heavens. In this character she came into contact from time to time not only with members of the Royal families of England and Germany, but with the leading astronomers of the age, who acknowledged in her an honoured comrade. A celebrated astronomer, referring to one of the many comets she was the first to discover, says in a letter to her: " I am more pleased than you can well conceive that you have made this discovery. You have immortalised your name, and you deserve such a reward from the Being who has ordered all these things to move as we find them, for your assiduity in the business of an astronomer, and for your love for so celebrated and deserving a brother."

As all the world knows, Mr. Herschel (then Sir William) was long recognised as the most celebrated astronomer of the time. And while none rejoiced more in his proud position than his sister, he was ever ready to acknowledge his indebtedness to her, as his companion in his herculean toils. The marvel is that the constant and exhausting strain of many long years did not prematurely wear out the strength and brain of both. They, however, grew old together, and alike lived to a remarkable old age. Sir William, who was twelve years the senior, was the first whose splendid constitution gave way. He died in the year 1822.

After her brother's death Miss Herschel, then in her 72nd year, seems to have felt unsettled in England and unable to face the scenes and life she had for so many years shared with her brother. Notwithstanding her attachment to her sister-in-law and her favourite nephew (who in some measure took the place in her affections of her beloved brother), she decided to return to Hanover. An absence of half a century from any place makes a wonderful difference in its associations, and Miss Herschel lived to regret her return to her native city, where, however, she resided for the remainder of her life. If her work by her brother's side was done, her long evening of life was, nevertheless, one of grateful recollection and laborious industry. Among other tasks, she undertook and completed a " Reduction and Arrangement, in the form of a catalogue in zones, of all the Star Clusters and Nebulæ observed by Sir W. Herschel in his Sweeps." For this she was, at a meeting of the Royal Astronomical Society in 1828, awarded the gold medal of the Society. The remarks made by Mr. South, the Vice-President, on that occasion, perhaps best summarise her great achievements. He said: "The labours of Miss Herschel are so intimately connected with, and are generally so dependent upon, those of her illustrious brother, that an investigation of the latter is absolutely necessary ere we can form the most remote idea of the extent of the former. But when it is considered that Sir W. Herschel's contributions to astronomical science occupy sixty-seven memoirs, communicated from time to time to the Royal Society, and embrace a period of forty years, it will not be expected that I should enter into their discussion. To the Philosophical Transactions I must refer you, and shall content myself with the hasty mention of some of her more immediate claims to the distinction now conferred. To deliver an eulogy, however deserved, upon *his* memory is not the purpose for which I am placed here. . . . But when we have thus enumerated the results obtained in the course of *sweeps* with this instrument, and taken into consideration the extent and variety of the other observations which were at the same time in progress, a most important part yet remains untold. Who participated in his toils? Who braved with him the inclemency of the weather? Who shared his privations? A female. Who was she? His sister. Miss Herschel it was who by *night* acted as his amanuensis; she it was whose pen conveyed to paper his observations as they issued from his lips; she it was who noted the night ascensions and polar distances of the objects observed; she it was who, having passed the night near the instrument, took the rough manuscripts to her cottage at the dawn of day, and produced a fair copy of the night's work on the following morning; she it was who planned the labour of each succeeding night; she it was who reduced every observation, made every calculation; she it was who arranged everything in systematic order; and she it was who helped him to obtain his imperishable name.

"But her claims to our gratitude do not end here. As an original observer she demands, and I am sure she has, our unfeigned thanks. Occasionally, her immediate attendance during the observations could be dispensed with. Did she pass the night in repose? No such thing. Wherever her brother was, there you were sure to find her. A sweeper planted on the lawn became her object of amusement; but her amusements were of the higher order, and to them we stand indebted for the discovery of the comet of 1786, of the comet of 1788, of the comet of 1791, of the comet of 1793, of the comet of 1795, since rendered familiar to us by the remarkable discovery of Encke. Many also of the nebulæ contained in Sir W. Herschel's catalogues were detected by her during these hours of enjoyment. Indeed, in looking at the joint labours of these extraordinary personages, we scarcely know whether most to admire the intellectual power of the brother, or the unconquerable industry of the sister."

A few years after this, in 1835, Miss Herschel was, along with Mrs. Somerville, made an Honorary Member of the Astronomical Society. The report of the council to the annual meeting contains the following well deserved words of praise:—

"Your Council has no small pleasure in recommending that the names of two ladies, distinguished in different walks of astronomy, be placed on the list of honorary members. On the propriety of such a step, in an astronomical point of view, there can be but one voice; and your Council is of opinion that the time has gone by when either feeling or prejudice, by whichever name it may be proper to call it, should be allowed to interfere with the payment of a well-earned tribute of respect.

Your Council has hitherto felt that, whatever might be its own sentiment on the subject, it had no right to place the name of a lady in a position the propriety of which might be contested, though upon what it might consider narrow grounds and false principles. But your Council has no fear that such a difference could now take place between any men whose opinion could avail to guide that of society at large; and, abandoning compliment on the one hand, and false delicacy on the other, submits, that while the tests of astronomical merit should in no case be applied to the works of a woman less severely than to those of a man, the sex of the former should no longer be an obstacle to her receiving any acknowledgment which may be held due to the latter. And your Council therefore recommends this meeting to add to the list of honorary members the names of Miss Caroline Herschel and Mrs. Somerville, of whose astronomical knowledge, and of the utility of the ends to which it has been applied, it is not necessary to recount the proofs."

Miss Herschel always maintained a warm correspondence with her relatives in England,

and when over eighty years of age wrote some recollections of her early years for her nephew. Notwithstanding her life of toil, she lived and retained her faculties to the wonderful age of ninety-seven years and ten months.

Her life affords an illustrious example of constant sisterly devotion from the days of lisping childhood, when her brother's love was her great joy, until when, after the lapse of almost a century—his memory her greatest happiness—she desired a lock of his hair to be placed in her coffin.

DOROTHY WORDSWORTH.

DOROTHY WORDSWORTH.

> Only a sister's part—yes, that was all;
>   And yet her life was bright, and full, and free.
> She did not feel, "I give up all for him";
>   She only knew, "'Tis mine his friend to be."

THE author of "Mornings in Spring" refers to Sir Philip and Mary Sidney as affording the most pleasing example of devotion between a brother and sister on record. He was probably correct in his estimate, for at the time when he wrote, the story of Dorothy Wordsworth was unknown. The opinion cannot, however, any longer be held. For among the fair cluster who in life's firmament hallow the sphere of sisterhood is one who must long claim the honoured place—Dorothy Wordsworth; look where we will, in her life she is the same, always loving, helpful, stimulating, inspiring, and faithful. The childhood's playmate feeds the brother's love, and becomes, even then, his "blessing." The very thought of the absent sister is like a "flash of light" cheering the loneliness of college chambers. The young woman stimulates the youthful poet, and calls back faith to the soul and hope to the despairing life, praises where others blame, with the prophetic eye of love divines the dormant power, and foresees the honoured future. Then follows the life-long companionship, involving for many years devoted service, both intellectual and household. For Dorothy Wordsworth was often the provider of subjects for her brother's poems, with diligent labour copied those poems, at the same time, by her reading and study, making herself his intellectual companion, and presiding over the household. And through all not the least part of her service lay in her complete self-effacement. With her intellectual endowment and rare literary skill she possessed the ability to have made herself no mean place in literature. All were surrendered in thought for the brother. Faithful Dorothy! Well might her brother love her with an almost unexampled love, this brightest example of sisterly devotion!

William and Dorothy Wordsworth were children of John Wordsworth, a solicitor practising in the quiet town of Cockermouth and agent of the then Earl of Lonsdale. Dorothy, who was the only daughter, was about a year and nine months younger than William, and was born on Christmas Day, 1771.

Circumstances sad in themselves not unfrequently tend to the development of latent character in a child; and to the surroundings of their earliest years and the influences then beginning to work we must look for the first germs from which was to spring the future harvest.

The loss of their mother when Dorothy was about six years old was the first of a succession of troubles which struck the lives of this brother and sister. This mother had been the centre of their home, the pivot round which their young lives turned. As Wordsworth afterwards said:—

>She was the heart
>And hinge of all our learning and our loves.

The little Dorothy was an impetuous, warm-hearted child, tender and loving, with the need of a home for the affections of her deep nature. With the loss of her mother she seems to have turned with an abandon of love to the brother next in age to herself. He was her playmate. The old garden with the terrace walk on the banks of the Derwent was the scene of many childish rambles and confidences. In later years, the poet in a few exquisite lines recalls the ministry of those early years. The flit of the butterfly brings to mind the time of many a childish gambol, the chief remembrance of which was the thought how she

>Feared to brush
>The dust from off its wings.

There, also, was the Sparrow's Dwelling:

>She looked at it, and seemed to fear it,
>Dreading, though wishing to be near it;
>Such heart was in her, being then
>A little Prattler among men.
>The Blessing of my later years
> Was with me when a boy:
>She gave me eyes, she gave me ears,
>And humble cares, and delicate fears,
>A heart, the fountain of sweet tears,
> And love, and thought, and joy.

Not long, however, after the death of their mother, William was sent to school at

Hawkshead, and Dorothy for a time lived with the father of her late mother at Penrith.

The death of their father, when Dorothy was about twelve years old, caused the entire break up of their early home, and from thence for some years their personal intercourse was only renewed at intervals. The father had not died in circumstances by any means affluent; but, through the kindness of prudent guardians, Wordsworth was enabled to finish his education at Cambridge. Dorothy meanwhile was passing her teens amid circumstances and scenes not the most congenial. Their absence from each other only stimulated their growing love. A visit to her during a vacation was to the brother blest

>   With a joy
> Above all joys, that seemed another morn
> Risen at mid noon; blessed with the presence
> Of that sole sister
> Now, after separation desolate,
> Restored to me—such absence that she seemed
> A gift then first bestowed.

Even now Dorothy was cherishing the design that she might become her brother's life companion. She looked forward to a time when they might be restored to each other—living loving life in a cottage, her brother great, she his servant and helper. This was the great hope that sustained her amidst present heart-yearning.

The history of Wordsworth about this time is now well known. College days over, an uncertainty of aim and purpose was the reason of his not fixing upon some occupation. His twelve months' residence in France during the period of the great Revolution did not assist in the solution of the problem of the young man's life, but only further entangled it. The outcome of the national struggle was bitterly disappointing to the enthusiastic English youth who had watched its progress with such keen interest. A change of rule was to be the dawn of hope to the nations. But when, instead of peace came strife and outrage, instead of prosperity misery, instead of freedom tyranny, instead of the fruition of hope the gloom of despair—then Wordsworth bowed his head in bitterness, ready almost to doubt the Almighty government of the world.

But the angel of his life came to his aid. Although their happiness was delayed, and Wordsworth's purposes remained unformed a year or two longer, the watchful love of his sister came as a soothing balm, and her dominant influence as a healing virtue. Friends blamed, but the sister confided, and encouraged her brother's desire to become a poet. Writing to a friend she says:

"William . . . has a sort of violence of affection—if I may so term it—which demonstrates itself every moment of the day, when the objects of his affection are present with him, in a thousand almost imperceptible attentions to their wishes, in a sort of restless watchfulness which I know not how to describe, a tenderness that never sleeps, and, at the same time, such a delicacy of manner as I have observed in few men." And again, " I am willing to allow that half the virtues with which I fancy him endowed are the creation of my love; but surely I may be excused! He was never afraid of comforting his sister; he never left her in anger; he always met her with joy; he preferred her society to every other pleasure—or, rather, when we were so happy as to be within each other's reach, he had no other pleasure when we were compelled to be divided."

What prevented now the carrying out of their long-formed project of living together was, unfortunately, their want of means. Without a profession for the brother, they appear to have been almost without income. But Providence gave what fortune withheld. The legacy of £900 bequeathed to Wordsworth by a friend whom he had nursed, and who recognised his genius, at length removed the cause which had kept the brother and sister apart. With scanty means, but overflowing love, they faced the world and conquered fate. The late Bishop of Lincoln, alluding to this period, says of Dorothy: "She was endowed with tender sensibility, with an exquisite perception of beauty, with a retentive recollection of what she saw, with a felicitous tact in discerning, and admirable skill in delineating natural objects with graphic accuracy and vivid gracefulness. She weaned him from contemporary politics, and won him to beauty and truth."

Wordsworth himself, the most reliable

informant as to what his sister did for him and
was to him, says:

> Depressed, bewildered thus, I did not walk
> With scoffers, seeking light and gay revenge
> From indiscriminate laughter, nor sit down
> In reconcilement with an utter waste
> Of intellect. . . .
>   Then it was—
> Thanks to the bounteous Giver of all good—
> That the beloved sister in whose sight
> Those days were passed, now speaking in a voice
> Of sudden admonition—like a brook
> That did but cross a lonely road, now
> Is seen, heard, felt, and caught at every turn,
> Companion never lost through many a league—
> Maintained for me a saving intercourse
> With my true self; for, though bedimmed and changed
> Much, as it seemed, I was no further changed
> Than as a clouded, and a waning moon;
> She whispered still that brightness would return.
> She, in the midst of all, preserved me still
> A poet; made me seek beneath that name,
> And that alone, my office upon earth.

The first home of William and Dorothy Wordsworth was at Racedown. Here their real life began for which their previous course had been a fitting preparation. Since the "home extinct" of their childhood they had both been more or less lonely; and now their dream was realised and their heart-yearning satisfied. It was not a life of idleness or self-indulgence. A singular similarity of taste and aim, added to the unusually strong natural affections, made existence for them a charm. Dorothy's strength of character is shown in the potent influence for good upon a nature like that of her brother. And she was as constant as faithful, as humble as powerful. Through a long life she never wavered; as year by year passed, her skill and judgment gaining maturity, her devotion appears in greater beauty.

It was while at Racedown that the friendship of Coleridge was made, a friendship close and lasting. For the sake of his companionship the Wordsworths soon went to reside at Alfoxden, in the neighbourhood of Nether Stowey. This proved to be a happy and fruitful period. The three poets (for Dorothy was essentially a poet) were almost inseparable, their rambles together by hill and combe and stream being followed by high discourse and mutual work in the dim lamplight. Here the Lyrical ballads were written.

Alfoxden did not, however, prove to be the poet's permanent home. After a residence there of about a little over a year, and a short period abroad, Wordsworth and his sister fixed upon the centre of England's lakeland as the scene of their future life. In the loved vale of Grasmere, on December 21, 1799, they took up their abode in the now famous Dove Cottage, a home of memories without peer.*

How the poet and his sister came to love their retreat among the mountains is well known. The few following years were among the most fruitful of his life. His best and most important work was there done. The humble cottage and "garden orchard" are not only immortalised in his verse, but were the scene of his loftiest labours. And Dorothy, meanwhile, not only inspired his ardour, fed both thought and pen, but laboured with her hands in the kitchen and at the desk. The following extract from the recently published *Recluse* (written at this time) not only shows

---

* Dove Cottage is now National property. For some years it was among the most treasured possessions of the present writer, who, at the solicitation of the Rev. Stopford Brooke and others, recently conveyed it for the purpose of a Wordsworth Memorial. It is now vested in Trustees on behalf of the public in a similar way to Shakespeare's birthplace at Stratford-on-Avon.

Wordsworth's satisfaction with his choice of residence, but his sustained feeling of his exceeding indebtedness to his sister :—

> Can the choice mislead,
> That made the calmest, fairest spot of earth,
> With all its unappropriated good,
> My own; and not mine only, for with me
> Entrenched, say rather peacefully embowered,
> Under yon orchard, in yon humble cot,
> A younger orphan of a home extinct,
> The only daughter of my parents dwells.
>   Aye, think on that, my heart, and cease to stir;
> Pause upon that, and let the breathing frame
> No longer breathe, but all be satisfied.
>   Oh, if such a silence be not thanks to God
> For what hath been bestowed, then where, where then
> Shall gratitude find rest? Mine eyes did ne'er
> Fix on a lovely object, nor my mind
> Take pleasure in the midst of happy thoughts,
> But either she whom now I have, who now
> Divides with me this loved abode, was there,
> Or not far off. Where'er my footsteps turned,
> Her voice was like a hidden bird that sang ;
> The thought of her was like a flash of light,
> Or an unseen companionship—a breath
> Of fragrance independent of the wind.
> In all my goings, in the new and old,
> Of all my meditations, and in this
> Favourite of all, in this the most of all.

Probably warmer and more loving praise was never bestowed or more happily expressed than is contained in these lines, unless, indeed, it be in the following, in which the poet, again alluding to his sister, speaks of the beneficent character of their intercourse :—

> She who dwells with me, whom I have loved
> With such communion, that no place on earth
> Can ever be a solitude to me. . . .

Once more, recounting in the "Prelude" the master influences which had entered into his life, prominent place is given to that exerted by his sister :—

> Child of my parents! Sister of my soul!
> Thanks in sincerest verse have been elsewhere
> Poured out for all the early tenderness
> Which I from thee imbibed; and 'tis most true
> That later seasons owed to thee no less;
> For, spite of thy sweet influence, and the touch
> Of kindred hands that opened out the springs
> Of genial thought in childhood, and in spite
> Of all that, unassisted, I had marked
> In life, or nature, of those charms minute,
> That win their way into the heart by stealth,
> Still, to the very going out of youth,
> I, too, exclusively esteemed *that* love,
> And sought *that* beauty, which, as Milton sings,
> Hath terror in it; but thou didst soften down
> This over sternness; but for thee, dear friend!
> My soul, too reckless of mild grace, had stood
> In her original self too confident,
> Retained too long a countenance severe;

> A rock with torrents roaring, with the clouds
> Familiar, and a favourite of the stars:
> But thou didst plant its crevices with flowers,
> Hang it with shrubs that twinkle in the breeze,
> And teach the little birds to build their nests
> And warble in its chambers. At a time
> When Nature, destined to remain so long
> Foremost in my affections, had fallen back
> Into a second place, pleased to become
> A handmaid to a nobler than herself,
> When every day brought with it some new sense
> Of exquisite regard for common things,
> And all the earth was budding with these gifts
> Of more refined humanity, thy breath,
> Dear sister, was a kind of gentler spring
> That went before my steps.

The marriage of Wordsworth, in 1802, did not occasion any waning of sympathy or cessation of intercourse between him and his sister. The circle was then only widened, not broken. Dorothy continued to be an honoured inmate of her brother's home, the sharer of his labours, and companion of his walks and excursions; in speech as well as in silence together garnering scenes of beauty and flowers of thought both for their own future lives and the world's weal. Thus the years passed with them calmly; each in its varying experiences of intense life—life haloed by the inward eye which glorifies the daily task, and finds in all Nature a fitting shrine—worth a decade of common days. It was a time of rare friendships also. It was by no means true of the Wordsworths that they withdrew themselves from the world in a selfish seclusion. Necessarily they were sensitive, and shunned the world's loud ways. If this had not been so we should never have had some of the finest poems in the language. To the humble cottage at Grasmere came, however, for treasured intercourse with the great master, many of the most gifted and cultured men of the time. But not for these only did Wordsworth live and write. He loved, and moved in and out among the sturdy and independent dalesmen among whom he had chosen to pass his life. There he found food for thought and pen, and perhaps never became grander in song or higher as a teacher than in delineating human life and nature as found in lowly homes.

As has been suggested, Miss Wordsworth might have earned for herself a place in literature had she not so entirely lived only for and in her brother. She was one of the most graceful and accomplished of letter writers; and the fragments from her journals, from time to time given to the world, written chiefly in the Alfoxden days and the early years at Grasmere, contain passages of rare beauty. To instance a few lines only. Alluding to a favourite birch tree, she says: "It was yielding to a gust of wind with all its tender twigs; the sun shone upon it, and it glanced in the wind like a flying sunshiny shower. It was a tree in shape, with stem and branches; but it was like a spirit of water." Recording one of her early visits with her brother to the Continent, she says : " Left London between five and six o'clock of the morning, outside the Dover coach. A beautiful morning. The city, St. Paul's, with the river—multitude of boats—made a beautiful sight as we crossed Westminster Bridge; the houses not overhung by their clouds of smoke, and were spread out endlessly, yet the sun shone so brightly, with such a pure light, that there was something like the purity of one of Nature's own grand spectacles. . . . Arrived at Calais at four in the morning. Delightful walks in the evening; seeing far off in the west the coast of England, like a cloud, crested with Dover Castle, the evening star and the glory of the sky; the reflections in the water were more beautiful than the sky itself; purple waves brighter than precious stones for ever melting away upon the sands." Deeply interesting as Miss Wordsworth's journals are, passages like these make us wish she had written more.

After between eight and nine years' residence in Grasmere, Miss Wordsworth accompanied her brother and his family on their removal to Rydal Mount. Here they lived for the remainder of their lives, and grew old together.

During many of their later years the life of the household was saddened and that of Miss Wordsworth darkened by the heavy affliction that came upon her. The exact date or occasion is somewhat doubtful, as well as to the extent to which Miss Wordsworth was afflicted. It was probably owing to her indefatigable exertions as a pedestrian in her intense love of Nature, and to want of sufficient care, that her splendid physical powers gave way. In 1832 she had an illness which resulted in brain fever, from the effects of which she never recovered. A few years later she became permanently invalided, and a long evening of life was passed more or less under a cloud. The present writer has the best of reasons for believing that the gravity of her mental condition during this period has been somewhat exaggerated. That the physical prostration became complete, and her keen mental powers sadly impaired, there is, unhappily, no doubt. But her affection of mind was chiefly shown by loss of memory; and her condition, even at the worst, was alleviated by many bright and lucid intervals. Her poem on "The Floating Island," written so late as 1842, is an abundant evidence of this.

In her suffering Miss Wordsworth was exemplary. To Wordsworth himself his sister's illness was a source of great sorrow. Remembering what she had been to him, we cannot wonder that, as Lady Richardson said of him : " There is always something touching in his way of speaking of his sister. The tones of his voice become very gentle and soothing."

Notwithstanding her long and sad affliction, Miss Wordsworth survived her brother five years. On account of her own condition, she was unable to be with him during his illness, and on being informed of his death, which took place on April 23, 1850, when she fully realised that " William " was no more, she exclaimed that life had nothing left worth living for. A friend who was present said, in reference to her: " She is drawn about as usual in her chair. She was heard to say, as she passed the door where the body lay, " O death, where is thy sting? O grave, where is thy victory?"

Miss Wordsworth's last years were tenderly cared for by those who had so long loved both her and her more famous brother. She died on January 25, 1855, in her eighty-third year. She is buried by her brother's side in Grasmere Churchyard.

MARY LAMB.

MARY LAMB.

IN the annals of domestic history it would be difficult to meet with a story more deeply interesting and pathetic than that of Charles and Mary Lamb. If Dorothy Wordsworth bears the palm for sisterly devotion and help, thereby crowning her brother's life with blessing, Charles Lamb stands before us the most signal example as the sharer and sustainer of a sister's lot of suffering. Darkest lives may be illumined by hope and brightened by love; and among lives of noble self-denial, those of Charles Lamb and his sister must always take a prominent place. Although they came into being heavily weighted for the race, their struggle with an adverse fate was noble, and the secret of their strength was their mutual love.

Probably no greater calamity can affect a family than an hereditary taint of insanity, entailing, as it does, such constant and tender care and infinite patience.

The father of Charles and Mary Lamb had been for many years a clerk to a barrister of the Inner Temple, in whose chambers, in Crown Office Row, he resided when Mary was born on December 3, 1764. There were other children of the family, none of whom, however, seem to have survived infancy with the exception of Mary, John, two years older, and Charles, ten years younger.

It would, perhaps, be difficult to imagine a more uncongenial home for a child constituted as was Mary Lamb than the one into which it was her lot to enter. We seek in vain in the immediate parentage of the Lambs for the many excellencies of character and the genius developed in both Mary and Charles. But one thing they both inherited from or through their father—the peculiarity of brain formation which renders its possessor liable to fits of madness. Little Mary was too loving for her early surroundings. Her parents seem to have lived to themselves, and not to have shown much love for the sensitive little one who, above all things, needed a heart-warm atmosphere.

Charles, writing of his mother, says that she "in feeling and sentiment and disposition bore so distant a resemblance to her daughter that she never understood her right—never could believe how much she loved her—but met her caresses, her protestations of filial affection, too frequently with coldness and repulse."

In her childhood Mary attended a day-school in Fetter Lane, where she received all the scholastic education she ever had. Her time was chiefly spent in the solitude of her own thoughts. A lonely childhood, however sad, is not infrequently beneficial in its results, in stimulating thought and bringing out the distinctive characteristics of a child. But to a child like Mary Lamb the very loneliness of her life would only tend to make more pronounced the liability to mental trouble. And although a taste for reading is one of the best that can be acquired, it would in the case of Mary Lamb have been all the better to have been carefully guarded and directed. It, however, afforded her no small delight to have the privilege of access to the library of her father's employer, "a spacious closet of good old English reading, where without much selection or prohibition she browsed at will upon that fair and wholesome pasturage."

A new element entered into the life of Mary when a little more than ten years of age. In the month of February, 1775, her brother Charles was born to feed the hunger of her loving heart. From the first he was her charge. She nursed the weakly child with tender care, fostered his loving disposition, and as she could, trained his infant mind. Their childhood thus passed hand in hand, in accord with their future lives.

When Charles was about seven years old he entered Christ's Hospital. It was here he first formed the friendship of Coleridge, which proved so fruitful in after years. As time passed over the household the circumstances of the Lambs, never affluent, became more straitened. The elder son, John, seems to have cared chiefly for himself, and not to have been very reliable for contribution to the family support. In his fifteenth year Charles left the Blue Coat School to bear his share (which proved to be a large one) of the burden of the family life. He obtained a clerkship in the South Sea House, which in two years was exchanged for a better one in the East India House, Mary at the same time also adding to the slender means by dressmaking.

A few years passed, not altogether without brightness, though much dimmed by the growing imbecility of the father, and the sickness and helplessness of the mother. In 1795 her father was pensioned by his kind old master, and the family removed into lodgings in Little Queen Street. The following year proved to the Lambs a disastrous one indeed. First Charles himself, from some immediate cause not very clear, became the victim of the fatal heritage. Mrs. Gilchrist suggests that it was the first and only love of which he was able to dream that " took deep hold of him, conspiring with the cares and trials of home life." Charles was, from whatever cause, for six weeks confined in an asylum. Writing to Coleridge, with whom he had kept up a constant intercourse, he says: "In your absence the tide of melancholy rushed in, and did its worst mischief by overwhelming my reason." It was during his confinement that, in one of his lucid intervals, he wrote the following sonnet to his sister:—

> If from my lips some angry accents fell,
> Peevish complaint, or harsh reproof unkind,
> 'Twas the error of a sickly mind
> And troubled thoughts, clouding the purer well,
> And waters clear of reason; and for me
> Let this my verse the poor atonement be—
> My verse, which thou to praise wert ere inclined
> Too highly, and with a partial eye to see
> No blemish. Thou to me didst ever show
> Kindest affection; and would ofttimes lend
> An ear to the desponding love-sick lay,
> Weeping my sorrows with me, and repay
> But ill the mighty debt of love I owe,
> Mary, to thee, my sister and my friend.

It was in the month of September in that year, a little while after the return of Charles to his home, that there occurred therein the saddest of domestic tragedies. The constant and increasing helplessness of the father and mother had necessitated no small amount of care and nursing on the part of Mary; following which had come the temporary madness of her brother, who had been to her a tower of strength and consolation. Finally selfish John, who generally lived from home at his ease, having met with an accident, had come home to be nursed, to be a further burden upon his much suffering sister—the last straw to the patient back. The unevenly balanced brain at last gave way, reason tottered, and in a fit of frenzy, Mary Lamb, the kind-hearted young woman, the loving daughter, the devoted sister, became the instrument of her mother's death. The *Weekly Register* contains the following account of the event :—

" This afternoon, the coroner's jury sat on the body of a lady in the neighbourhood of Holborn, who died in consequence of a wound from her daughter, the preceding day. While the family were preparing dinner, the young lady, in a fit of insanity, seized a case-knife lying on the table, and in a menacing manner pursued a little girl, her apprentice, round the room. On the eager calls of her helpless, infirm mother to forbear, she renounced her first object, and, with loud shrieks, approached her parent. The child, by her cries, quickly brought up the landlord* of the house—but too late. The dreadful scene presented to him

* This appears to be a mistake. It was Charles himself who performed the sad duty of overpowering his sister.

the mother lifeless on a chair; her daughter yet wildly standing over her with the fatal knife ; and the venerable old man—her father —weeping by her side, himself bleeding at the forehead from the effects of a blow he received from one of the forks she had been madly hurling about the room. But a few days prior to this, the family had discovered some symptoms of lunacy in her, which had so much increased on the Wednesday evening that her brother early the next morning went in quest of Dr. Pitcairn ; had that gentleman been providentially met with, the fatal catastrophe had, probably, been prevented. She had once before, in the earlier part of her life, been deranged from the harassing fatigues of too much business. As her carriage towards her mother had been ever affectionate in the extreme, it is believed that to her increased attentiveness to her is to be ascribed the loss of her reason at this time. The jury, without hesitation, brought in their verdict—Lunacy."

From the fatal hour when Mary lifted her hand against her mother, to the last of his life, Charles Lamb was heroic in his self-denying devotion to her. As a matter of course, she had to be, for the time being, placed under restraint. But Charles then and there, in his noble love and sense of duty, determined that, abandoning all other loves and hopes which might interfere with his one great, self-imposed purpose, his life should be devoted to the welfare and care of his sister. A few days after the occurrence, he wrote to his friend Coleridge :—

"My poor dear, dearest sister, in a fit of insanity has been the death of her own mother. I was at hand only in time enough to snatch the knife out of her grasp. She is at present in a madhouse, from whence I fear she must be moved to a hospital. God has preserved to me my senses; I eat and drink, and sleep, and have my judgment, I believe, very sound. My poor father was slightly wounded, and I am left to take care of him and my aunt. Mr. Norris, of the Blue Coat School, has been very kind to us, and we have no other friend; but, thank God, I am very calm and composed, and able to do the best that remains to do. Write as religious a letter as possible, but no mention of what is gone and done with. With me " the former things are passed away," and I have something more to do than to feel. God Almighty have us all in His keeping! Mention nothing of poetry. I have destroyed every vestige of past vanities of that kind. . . . Your judgment will convince you not to take any notice of this yet to your dear wife. You look after your family; I have my reason and strength left to take care of mine. I charge you do not think of coming to see me. Write. I will not see you if you come. God Almighty love you and all of us!"

Coleridge's reply was full of comfort to his afflicted friend, and upon its receipt Charles writes again:—

"Your letter was an inestimable treasure to me. It will be a comfort to you, I know, to know that our prospects are somewhat better. My poor dear, dearest sister, the unhappy and unconscious instrument of the Almighty's judgment on our house is restored to her senses, to a dreadful sense and recollection of what has passed, awful to her mind, and impressive (as it must be to the end of life), but tempered with religious resignation and the reasonings of a sound judgment, which in this early stage knows how to distinguish between the deed committed in a transient fit of frenzy and the terrible guilt of a mother's murder. I have seen her. I found her this morning calm and serene: far, very far, from an indecent, forgetful serenity. She has a most affectionate and tender concern for what has happened. Indeed, from the beginning, frightful and hopeless as her disorder seemed, I had confidence enough in her strength of mind and religious principle, to look forward to a time when even she might recover tranquility. God be praised, Coleridge, wonderful as it is to tell, I have never been otherwise than collected and calm; even on the dreadful day and in the midst of the terrible scene, I preserved a tranquility which bystanders may have construed into indifference—a tranquility not of despair. Is it folly or sin in me to say that it was a religious principle that most supported me? I allow much to other favourable circumstances. I felt that I had something else to do than to regret. On that first evening my aunt was lying insensible—to all appearance like one dying; my father, with his poor forehead plastered over from the wound he had received from a daughter, dearly loved by him, and who loved him no less dearly; my mother a dead and murdered corpse in the next room; yet was I wonderfully supported. I closed not my eyes in sleep that night, but lay without terrors and without despair. I have lost no sleep since. I had been long used not to rest in things of sense; had endeavoured after a comprehension of mind unsatisfied with the "ignorant present time," and this kept me up. I had the whole weight of the family thrown on me; for my brother, little disposed (I speak not without tenderness for him) at any time to take care of old age and infirmities, had now, with his bad leg, an exemption from such duties, and I was left alone. One little incident may serve to make you understand my way of managing my mind. Within a day or two after the fatal one, we dressed for dinner a tongue, which we had had salted for some weeks in the house. As I sat down, a feeling like remorse struck me; this tongue poor Mary got for me, and can I partake of it now when she is far away? A thought occurred and relieved me: if I give in to this way of feeling there is not a chair, a room, an object in our rooms, that will not awaken our keenest griefs. I must rise above such weaknesses. I hope this was not want of true feeling. I do not let this carry me, though, too far. On the very second day (I date from the day of horrors) as is usual in such cases, there was a matter of twenty people, I do think, supping in our room; they prevailed on me to eat with them (for to eat I never refused). They were all making merry in the room! Some had come from friendship, some from busy curiosity, and some from interest. I was going to partake with them, when my recollection came that my poor dead mother was lying in the next room—a mother who, through life, wished nothing but her children's welfare. Indignation, the rage of grief, something like remorse, rushed upon my mind. In any agony of emotion, I found my way mechanically into an adjoining room, and fell on my knees by the side of her coffin, asking forgiveness of heaven, and sometimes of her, for forgetting her so soon. Tranquility returned, and it was the only violent emotion that mastered me. I think it did me good. . . .

" She will [referring to Mary], I fancy, if she stays, make one of the family rather than of the patients; and the old and young ladies I like exceedingly, and she loves them dearly; and they, as the saying is, take to her very extraordinarily—if it is extraordinary that people who see my sister should love her. Of all the people I ever saw in the world, my poor sister was most and thoroughly devoid of the least tincture of selfishness .... and if I mistake not, in the most trying situation that a human being can be found in, she will be found (I speak not with sufficient humility, I fear) but humanly and foolishly speaking, she will be found, I trust, uniformly great and amiable. . . ."

His next letter reveals something of the sister's state of feeling under the distressing circumstances.

"Mary continues serene and cheerful. I find by me a little letter she wrote to me; for though I see her almost every day, yet we delight to write to one another, for we can scarce see each other but in company with some of the people of the house. I have not the letter by me, but will quote from memory what she wrote in it: 'I have no bad, terrifying dreams. At midnight, when I happen to awake, the nurse sleeping by the side of me, with the noise of the poor mad people around me, I have no fear. The spirit of my mother seems to descend and smile upon me, and bid me live to enjoy the life and reason which the Almighty has given me. I shall see her again in heaven; she will then understand me better. My grandmother, too, will understand me better, and will then say no more, as she used to do, 'Polly, what are those poor, crazy, moythered brains of yours thinking of always?'"

In another letter he says: "I am wedded, Coleridge, to the fortunes of my sister and my poor old father.... What would I give to call her back to earth for one day? on my knees to ask her pardon for all those little asperities of temper, which from time to time have given her gentle spirit pain? and the day, my friend, I trust, will come. There will be time enough for kind offices of love, if heaven's eternal year be ours. Hereafter her meek spirit shall not reproach me."

Mary, on this first occasion, remained in the asylum at Islington for some months. Eventually, upon the solemn promise of her brother that for his life she should be under his especial care, he was permitted to take her under his own protection. He did not, however, remove her at once to his own home, but provided for her in lodgings at Hackney. Alluding to her at this time, he writes : " To get her out into the world again, with a prospect of her never being so ill again, this is to be ranked not upon the common blessings of Providence. May that merciful God make tender my heart and make me as thankful as, in my distress, I was earnest in my prayers ! "

The fond hope of Lamb, that his sister would never be so ill again, was not destined to be fulfilled. By the end of the year she was again in the asylum, but always in her brother's thought. During her absence he thus gave utterance to his thoughts:—

> I am a widowed thing now thou art gone!
> Now thou art gone, my own familiar friend,
> Companion, sister, helpmate, counsellor!
> Alas! that honoured mind, whose sweet reproof
> And meekest wisdom in times past have smoothed
> The unfilial harshness of my foolish speech,
> And made me loving to my parents old
> (Why is this so; ah, God! why is this so?)
> That honoured mind become a fearful blank,
> Her sense locked up, and herself kept out

From human sight or converse, while so many
Of the foolish sort are left to roam at large,
Do all acts of folly and sin and shame!
Thy paths are mystery!
    Yet I will not think
Sweet friend, but we shall one day meet and live
In quietness, and die so, fearing God;
Or if not—and these false suggestions be
A fit of the weak nature, loath to part
With what it loved so long and held so dear,—
If thou art to be taken and I left
(More sinning, yet unpunished save in thee),
It is the will of God, and we are clay
In the Potter's hand, and at the worst are made
From absolute nothing, vessels of disgrace,
Till His most righteous purpose wrought in us,
Our purified spirits find their perfect rest.

It was not until the death of his father, in the early part of 1799, that Charles felt it desirable to take his sister to his own home. At this time Mary was thirty-five and Charles twenty-five. From this time forward they were, indeed, one. They lived and worked together, thought together, and side by side grew old. They had several changes of residence—always in London or the suburbs. Mary had also many relapses. Both knew she was liable to them, and they lived always on the brink of this great trouble. As for Lamb himself, he was never again subject to the terrible malady. He had no time for brooding. The constant thought required for his sister made him strong—forced him to brace himself to face the stern duty whenever required. And Mary herself fronted the sadness of her lot with fortitude. In preparation for any short holiday together, which they occasionally made, she would with her own hands pack as a necessary article of luggage the strait jacket, which might at any moment be required for use upon herself. There is no picture more pathetic than that presented of this loving brother and sister, how that, after a premonition of the on-coming affliction, they would set out, hand in hand, for her temporary asylum, together weeping over the sadness of their lot. And this continued throughout their lives.

And yet it would be wrong to suppose their path to have been altogether sad. It was illumined by love, the heavy load was lightened by mutual help. Their devotion to each other, and joint pursuit of literature, was an immense compensation in their hard fate, bringing, as it ever does, the ideal into the actual, and casting a glamour of romance over the most heart-breaking realities of existence.

They had also many friends—friends after their own heart—who loved the intellectual converse of their humble home, and who knew well the circumstances of their saddened lives. These would include from time to time many of the choicest spirits of the age, whom the genius and gentleness of Lamb brought to his side. Barry Cornwall, in his memoir, says:—

"Lamb and his sister had an open party once a week, every Wednesday evening, where his friends generally went to visit him, without any special invitation. He invited you suddenly, not pressingly; but with such heartiness that you at once agreed to come. There was usually a game at whist on these evenings, in which the stakes were very moderate, indeed, almost nominal. When my thoughts turn backward, as they sometimes do, to those past days, I see my dear old friend again—'in my mind's eye, Horatio'—with his outstretched hand, and his grave, sweet smile of welcome. It was always in a room of moderate size, comfortably, but plainly furnished, that he lived. An old mahogany table was opened out in the middle of the room, round which, and near the walls, were old highbacked chairs (such as our grandfathers used), and a long plain bookcase completely filled with old books. These were his 'ragged veterans.' Here Charles Lamb sat, when at home, always near the table. At the opposite side was his sister, engaged in some domestic work, knitting or sewing, or poring over a modern novel. 'Bridget in some things is behind her years.' In fact, although she was ten years older than her brother, she had more sympathy with modern books and with youthful fancies than he had. She wore a neat cap of the fashion of her youth, and an old-fashioned dress. Her face was pale and somewhat square, but very placid, with grey, intelligent eyes. She was very mild in her manner to strangers, and to her brother gentle and tender always. She had often an upward look of peculiar meaning when directed towards him, as though to give him assurance that all was then well with her. His affection for her was somewhat less on the surface, but always present. There was great gratitude intermingled with it. 'In the days of weakling infancy,' he writes, 'I was her tender charge, as I have been her care in foolish manhood since.' Then he adds pathetically, 'I wish I could throw into a heap the remainder of our joint existences, that we might share them in equal division.'"

Mrs. Cowden Clarke has also left some very interesting reminiscences of this period. She says:—

" Miss Lamb bore a strong personal resemblance to her brother, being in stature under middle height, possessing well-cut features, and a countenance of singular sweetness, with intelligence. Her brown eyes were soft, yet penetrating, her nose and mouth very shapely; while the general expression was mildness itself. She had a speaking voice, gentle and persuasive; and her smile was her brother's own—winning in the extreme. There was a certain catch, or emotional breathingness, in her utterance, which gave an inexpressible charm to her reading of poetry, and which lent a captivating earnestness to her mode of speech when addressing those she liked. This slight check, with its yearning, eager effect in her voice, had something softendly akin to her brother Charles's impediment of articulation ; in him it scarcely amounted to a stammer; in her it merely imparted additional stress to the fine-sensed suggestions she made to those whom she counselled or consoled. She had a mind at once nobly toned and practical, making her ever a chosen source of confidence among her friends, who turned to her for consultation, confirmation, and advice in matters of nicest moment—always secure of deriving from her both aid and solace. Her manner was easy, almost homely, so quiet, unaffected, and perfectly unpretending was it. Beneath the sparing talk and retiring carriage few casual observers would have suspected the ample information and large intelligence that lay comprised there. She was oftener a listener than a speaker. In the modest-'havioured woman simply sitting there, taking small share in general conversation, few, who did not know her, would have imagined the accomplished classical scholar, the excellent understanding, the altogether rarely-gifted being, moral and mental, that Mary Lamb was. Her apparel was always of the plainest kind—a black stuff or silk gown, made and worn in the simplest fashion conceivable. She took snuff liberally—a habit that had evidently grown out of her propensity to sympathise with and share her brother's tastes; and it certainly had the effect of enhancing her likeness to him. She had a small, white, and delicately-formed hand; and as it hovered above the tortoiseshell box containing the powder so strongly approved by them both, in search of a stimulating pinch, the act seemed yet another link of association between the brother and sister when hanging together over their favourite books and studies."

During all the time of periodic distress both Charles and Mary Lamb were, from time to time, engaged in literary work. In the quiet home, the most liable among tens of thousands to be at any moment the scene of heartrending upheaval, we should not have looked for some of the best work of the age. But such was the case. In the most devoted brother of the century we have, at the same time, the quaintest humourist and one of the most subtle critics. And in Mary herself we have a striking instance of scholastic training being supplemented by home study and wide reading, until she became an accomplished scholar and a fit companion to her greater brother. Probably, her love for him was the great moving cause of Mary's culture. Her own contributions to literature were of no slight value and interest. Of the twenty ever-favourite "Tales from Shakespeare," fourteen were written by Mary, the six tragedies being the production of Charles. The tales are written with the felicity of style peculiar to the Lambs, and form a suitable introduction, especially for young people, to the works of the great dramatist. In a letter by Mary, referring to this joint production, she says: "Charles has written 'Macbeth,' 'Othello,' 'King Lear,' and has begun 'Hamlet.' You would like to see us, as we often sit writing on one table (but not on one cushion, sitting like Hermia and Helena in the *Midsummer Night's Dream*), or, rather, like an old literary Darby and Joan—I taking snuff, and he groaning all the while, and saying he can make nothing of it, which he always says till he has finished, and then he finds out that he has made something of it." Mary also wrote a series of entertaining stories for children under the title of " Mrs. Leicester's School." Nor did she confine herself to prose. She was the author of several of the pieces in " Poetry for Children," published in the names of her brother and herself. It is not certain which of the poems are hers. Apart from authentic information, of which there is none, opinion is speculative. Charles stated that his own was about one-third of the whole.

Mary was to her friends a generous correspondent. Her letters show the same ease and gracefulness of style as the " Tales," and are very pleasant reading. As a sample one may be given, written to Dorothy Wordsworth, shortly after the loss of her brother, Captain Wordsworth, in the *Abergavenny*. This gives us a glimpse of the writer's sympathetic heart and rare sensibility—

" I thank you, my kind friend, for your most comfortable letter; till I saw your own handwriting I could not persuade myself that I should do well to write to you, though I have often attempted it; but I always left off dissatisfied with what I had written, and feeling that I was doing an improper thing to intrude upon your sorrow. I wished to tell you that you would one day feel the kind of peaceful state of mind and sweet memory of the dead which you so happily describe as now almost beginning; but I felt that it was improper and most grating to the feelings of the afflicted to say to them that the memory of their affliction would in time become a constant part, not only of their dream, but of their most wakeful sense of happiness. That you would see every object with and through your lost brother, and that that would at last become a real and everlasting source of comfort to you, I felt and well knew, from my own experience in sorrow; but till you yourself began to feel this I did not dare tell you so; but I send you some poor lines which I wrote under this conviction of mind, and before I heard Coleridge was returning home. I will transcribe them now, before I finish my letter, lest a false shame prevent me then, for I know they are much worse than they ought to be, written as they were with strong feeling, and on such a subject; every line seems to me to be borrowed; but I had no better way of expressing my thoughts, and I never have the power of altering or amending anything I have once laid aside with dissatisfaction :—

> " Why is he wandering on the sea ?
> Coleridge should now with Wordsworth be.
> By slow degrees he'd steal away
> Their woe, and gently bring a ray
> (So happily he'd time relief)
> Of comfort from their very grief.
> He'd tell them that their brother, dead,
> When years have passèd o'er their head,
> Will be remembered with such holy,
> True, and perfect melancholy,
> That ever this lost brother John
> Will be their heart's companion.
> His voice they'll always hear,
> His face they'll always see,
> There's naught in life so sweet
> As such a memory."

When Miss Wordsworth's reply to this consoling letter arrived, it devolved upon Charles to answer it for the sad reason stated. He writes (June 14, 1805):—" Your long, kind letter has not been thrown away, for it has given me great pleasure to find you are all resuming your old occupations and are better; but poor Mary, to whom it is addressed, cannot yet relish it. She has been attacked with one of her severe illnesses and is at present from home. Last Monday week was the day she left me, and I hope I may calculate upon having her again in a month or little more. I am rather afraid late hours have, in this case, contributed to her indisposition. . . . I have every reason to suppose that this illness, like all the former ones, will be but temporary ; but I cannot always feel so. In the meantime she is dead to me, and I miss a prop. All my strength is gone, and I am like a fool bereft of her co-operation. I dare not think, lest I should think wrong, so used am I to look up to her in the least as in the biggest perplexity. To say all I know of her would be more than I think anybody could believe or even understand ; and when I hope to have her well again with me, it would be sinning against her feelings to go about to praise her, for I can conceal nothing that I do from her. She is older and wiser and better than I, and all my wretched imperfections I cover to myself by resolutely thinking of her goodness. She would share life and death, heaven and hell with me. She lives but for me, and I know I have been wasting and teasing her life for five years past incessantly with my cursed drinking and ways of going on. But even in this upbraiding of myself I am offending against her, for I know that she has clung to me for better for worse; and if the balance has been against her hitherto it was a noble trade. . . ."

The death of Coleridge, in 1834, was a great bereavement to the Lambs. Charles seems to have lived under a constant sense of personal loss. In six months he followed his friend to the unseen world. The fond desire of the brother and sister that she should die first was thus unfulfilled; but she was becoming more and more cut off from the realities of life, and probably hardly ever realised the bitterness of the separation. Wordsworth wrote a poem to the memory of Lamb containing feeling allusions to Mary. In reference to it he said: "Were I to give way to my own feelings, I should dwell not only on her genius and intellectual powers, but upon the delicacy and refinement of manner which she maintained inviolable under most trying circumstances. She was loved and honoured by all her brother's friends; and others, some of them strange characters, whom his philanthropic peculiarities induced him to countenance."

Thou wert a scorner of the fields, my friend,
But more in show than truth; and from the fields,
And from the mountains, to thy rural grave
Transported, my soothed spirit hovers o'er
Its green, untrodden turf, and blowing flowers;
And taking up a voice shall speak (though still
Awed by the theme's peculiar sanctity
Which words less free presumed not even to touch)
Of that fraternal love, whose heaven-lit lamp
From infancy, through manhood, to the last
Of threescore years, and to thy latest hour,
Burnt on with ever-strengthening light, enshrined
Within thy bosom.

     "Wonderful" hath been
The love established between man and man,
"Passing the love of women;" and between
Man and his helpmate in fast wedlock joined
Through God, is raised a spirit and soul of love
Without whose blissful influence Paradise
Had been no Paradise; and earth were now
A waste where creatures bearing human form,
Direst of savage beasts would roam in fear,
Joyless and comfortless. Our days glide on;
And let him grieve who cannot choose but grieve
That he hath been an elm without his vine,
And her bright dower of clustering charities,
That, round his trunk and branches, might have clung
Enriching and adorning. Unto thee,
Not so enriched, not so adorned, to thee
Was given (say rather, thou of later birth,
Wert given to her) a sister—'tis a word
Timidly uttered, for she lives, the meek,
The self-restraining, and the ever kind;

In whom thy reason and intelligent heart
Found, for all interests, hopes, and tender cares,
All softening, humanising, hallowing powers,
Whether withheld, or for her sake unsought—
More than sufficient recompense!

                       Her love
(What weakness prompts the voice to tell it here?)
Was as the love of mothers; and when years,
Lifting the boy to man's estate, had called
The long-protected to assume the part
Of a protector, the first filial tie
Was undissolved; and, in or out of sight,
Remained imperishably interwoven
With life itself.
     .   .   .   .   .

O gift divine of quiet sequestration!
The hermit exercised in prayer and praise,
And feeding daily on the hope of heaven,
Is happy in his vow, and fondly cleaves
To life-long singleness; but happier far
Was to your souls, and, to the thoughts of others,
A thousand times more beautiful appeared,
Your dual loneliness. The sacred tie
Is broken; yet, why grieve? for Time but holds
His moiety in trust, till Joy shall lead
To the blest world where parting is unknown.

Mary survived her brother for thirteen years, being lovingly cared for in the twilight of her life by sympathising friends. She died in May, 1847; and they now rest in the same grave in Edmonton churchyard.

ELIZABETH H. WHITTIER.

ELIZABETH H. WHITTIER.

READERS of Whittier, the now venerable and famous American poet, will remember fond allusions to his favourite sister Elizabeth, who during her life was a bright and stimulating member of the poet's earlier and later home. The day has not yet come when we can learn much of her happy influence upon him. She was pre-eminently her brother's sister, and of her character as such we cannot now know much. She was also herself a poet, and several of her pieces have been published. A few particulars of her life cannot be uninteresting.

She was born on December 7, 1815, the younger sister of the poet, being the fourth and last child of their father, John Whittier. Elizabeth derived her second name from the family of her mother, whose maiden name was Abigail Hussey, and who was of English descent. The Whittiers had for some generations lived in a house built by one of the ancestors of the family at Haverill, and had been prominent members of the Society of Friends.

The young Whittiers were happy in their parenthood, as well as in their early surroundings. Their father was an honest, upright, sturdy yeoman, to whom a mean and cowardly action was unknown, while their mother was gifted with the natural refinement of thought and manner distinguishing the possession of a gentle heart.

Passages in Whittier's "Snowbound" are pleasantly descriptive of his early home and its members. Of his mother he writes:—

> Our mother, while she turned her wheel,
> Or run the new-knit stocking heel,
> Told how the Indian hordes came down
> At midnight on Cochico town.
> Then haply, with a look more grave,
> And soberer tone, some tale she gave
> From painful Sewall's ancient tome,
> Beloved in every Quaker home,
> And faith fire-winged by martyrdom.

Of his sister Mary he says:—

> There, too, our elder sister plied
> Her evening task the stand beside;

> A full, rich nature, free to trust,
> Truthful and almost sternly just,
> Impulsive, earnest, prompt to act,
> And make her generous thought a fact,
> Keeping with many a light disguise,
> The secret of self-sacrifice.

And thus of Elizabeth :—

> As one who held herself a part
> Of all she saw, and let her heart
> Against the household bosom lean,
> Upon the motley braided mat
> Our youngest and our dearest sat,
> Lifting her large, sweet, asking eyes.

When Elizabeth was born, John, the future poet, was just eight years old, and attending his first school. Years wore on, and the boy's occupation alternated between school, household duties, and work on his father's farm. Meanwhile his little sister was, from the exemplary household gathered under her father's roof, and the sweet influences of a happy home, receiving the impressions and learning the precious lessons which can only be gathered during the earliest years, and through which the little human child becomes the sweetest thing in life.

Whilst Elizabeth was still a child a leading

incident in the boy's life took place. His old schoolmaster, on paying a visit to his father's house, brought a copy of the poems of Burns, from which he recited certain pieces, greatly to the delight of John, who borrowed the book. He adds:—" This was about the first poetry I had ever read (with the exception of that of the Bible, of which I had been a close student), and it had a lasting influence upon me. I began to make rhymes myself, and to imagine stories and adventures." So we find the boy of fourteen beginning to write his first poems, which, under the encouragement of his elder sister Mary, he continued to do for some years, when he began to send anonymous contributions from his pen to the local newspaper. He was only a country youth, working in his father's fields; but by thoughtful sympathy Nature had become glorified for him, and life was soon to be sanctified. Notice was taken of his poetical productions, he was stimulated to greater exertion, and through his own industry obtained the means of attending the Haverhill Academy for a short period when in his twentieth year. The next few years of the future poet's life were spent between his own schooling, teaching others, helping on the farm, and editing and contributing to country newspapers.

But if it were the elder sister who encouraged Whittier in his earliest poetic efforts, it was Elizabeth who became more and more, with her growing years, his "heart's companion," his imitator, his *alter ego*. We learn from one of his letters during a visit which he paid to his home in 1831, that Elizabeth, then a girl of fifteen summers, had herself begun to write verses. The following are the opening lines of a description by her of "Autumn Sunset":—

O, there is beauty in the sky—a widening of gold
Upon each light and breezy cloud, and on each vapoury
    fold!
The Autumn wind has died away, and the air has not a
    sound,
Save the sighing of the withered leaves as they fall
    upon the ground.

During this visit to his home Whittier's father died. This circumstance probably influenced him in his decision to resign his position as editor of *The New England Weekly Review*, that he might return to his mother and sisters.

One pleasing glimpse we catch of Elizabeth in her twentieth year. Sharing her brother's anti-slavery sympathies, she was occasionally called to share the dangers which at that time beset those who had the courage to espouse the cause of the oppressed. In 1835, when Whittier was the corresponding secretary of the Anti-slavery Society of Haverhill, a lecture on slavery having been announced was interfered with by the mob, who terrified the audience by a disgraceful attack upon the building where the lecture was being delivered. The meeting was broken up in confusion, and it was in part owing to the bravery of Miss Whittier that the lecturer escaped in safety, she, along with another young lady, undertaking to escort the lecturer, pushing their way through the threatening mob. On another occasion, when attending a meeting of the Female Anti-slavery Society at Boston, Elizabeth was herself in considerable danger of rough usage at the hands of her infuriated opponents. She did not by any means lead a public life, but was, on the contrary, of a retiring and gentle nature, and it was only the cruel wrongs of the oppressed that roused her sympathies and led her to active endeavours on their behalf.

In the year 1840 the farm at Haverhill passed out of the family, and they removed to Amesbury. It then consisted of four members only—the poet and his mother, aunt, and sister Elizabeth.

Thenceforth, until her death, she was her brother's close companion. The playmate of his childhood became the adviser of his riper years, the sharer of his sympathies, hopes, and aims. Happy lives are generally uneventful, except, indeed, in what constitutes their best portion—the pleasant intercourse, the loving ministries which go to make life so truly worth living.

With such inmates we are sure that the poet's home at Amesbury was supremely blessed—that the years passed gently and time touched kindly. But the happy circle gradually thinned. A few years after settling at Amesbury the cherished aunt died; some years later—in 1857—the mother. From thenceforth until her own death in 1864, Elizabeth seems to have been her brother's sole companion.

When Whittier's sister died her memory

lived. The empty home seems to have carried back his mind to his earlier home in the quiet valley where his sister shared his woodland rambles, and where the icy grasp of winter imprisoned the complete family round the glowing hearth. It was in the year following his sister's death Whittier wrote the poem before referred to, " Snowbound," which is at once fondly reminiscent of bygone days and touched with a tender memory of his latest loss. He says :—

> As one who held herself a part
> Of what she saw, and let her heart
>   Against the household bosom lean,
> Upon the motley-braided mat
> Our youngest and our dearest sat,
> Lifting her large, sweet, asking eyes,
>   Now bathed within the fadeless green
> And holy peace of Paradise.
> Oh, looking from some heavenly hill,
>   Or from the shade of saintly palms,
>   Or silver reach of river calms,
> Do those large eyes behold me still?
> With me one little year ago—
> The chill weight of the winter snow
>   For months upon her grave has lain:
> And now, when summer south winds blow
>   And brier and harebell bloom again,
> I tread the pleasant paths we trod,
> I see the violet-sprinkled sod

Whereon she leaned, too frail and weak
The hillside flowers she loved to seek,
Yet following me where'er I went
With dark eyes full of love's content.
The birds are glad; the brier-rose fills
The air with sweetness; all the hills
Stretch green to June's unclouded sky;
But still I wait with ear and eye
For something gone which should be nigh,
A loss in all familiar things,
In flower that blooms, and bird that sings.
And yet, dear heart, remembering thee,
    Am I not richer than of old?
Safe in thy immortality,
    What change can reach the wealth I hold?
    What chance can mar the pearl and gold
Thy love hath left in trust for me?
And while in life's late afternoon,
    Where cool and long the shadows grow,
I walk to meet the night that soon
    Shall shape and shadow overflow,
I cannot feel that thou art far,
Since near at need the angels are;
And when the sunset gates unbar,
    Shall I not see thee waiting stand,
And, white against the evening star,
    The welcome of thy beckoning hand?

But Miss Whittier's influence did not cease with her death. How much her brother missed her no one will ever know. He had been accustomed to consult her, and to value her opinion. In his next published poem,

"The Tent on the Beach," he refers regretfully to the

> Memory of one who might have tuned my song
> To sweeter music by her delicate ear.

But the sister's influence was felt not only in the sweet sadness which such a memory casts over a life. As a poet Whittier was enabled to proceed to still greater heights. Her loss did not check his zeal or stay his pen, but only softened and toned his utterance by the mellowing and purifying influence of tender recollection.

In 1875, when Whittier published his "Hazel Blossoms," he was induced to include in the volume several of the poems of his sister. The poems are "The Dream of Argyle," "Dr. Kane in Cuba," "The Wedding Veil," "The Meeting Waters," "Charity," "Lines written on the Departure of Joseph Sturge after his Visit to the Abolitionists of the United States," and "Lady Franklin." In a note Whittier says: "I have ventured, in compliance with the desire of dear friends of my beloved sister Elizabeth H. Whittier, to add to this little volume the few poetical pieces which she left behind her. As she was very distrustful of her powers, and altogether without ambition for literary distinction, she shunned everything like publicity, and found far greater happiness in generous appreciation of the gifts of her friends than in the gratification of her own. Yet it has always seemed to me that had her health, sense of duty and fitness, and her extreme self-distrust permitted, she might have taken high place among lyrical singers. These poems, with perhaps two or three exceptions, afford but slight indications of the life of the writer, who had an almost morbid dread of spiritual and literary egotism, or of her tenderness of sympathy, chastened mirthfulness, and pleasant play of thought and fancy, when her shy, beautiful soul opened like the flower in the warmth of social communion. In the lines on Dr. Kane her friends will see something of her fine individuality—the rare mingling of of delicacy and intensity of feeling which made her dear to them. This little poem reached Cuba while the great explorer lay on his death-bed, and we are told that he listened with grateful tears while it was read to him by his mother.

"I am tempted to say more, but I write as under the eye of her who, while with us, shrank with painful deprecation from the praise or mention of performances which seemed so far below her ideal of excellence."

As this little poem, " Dr. Kane in Cuba," is rendered doubly interesting by the above-mentioned pathetic incident, it is given along with the one which follows in illustration of Miss Whittier's writing :—

Dr. Kane in Cuba.

A noble life is in thy care,
    A sacred trust to thee is given ;
Bright island ! Let the healing air
    Be to him as the breath of heaven.

The marvel of his daring life—
    The self-forgetting leader bold—
Stirs, like the trumpet's call to strife,
    A million hearts of meaner mould.

Eyes that shall never meet his own
    Look dim with tears across the sea,
Where from the dark and icy zone,
    Sweet isle of flowers ! he comes to thee.

Fold him in rest, O pitying clime !
    Give back his wasted strength again·
Soothe with thy endless summer time,
    His winter-wearied heart and brain.

Sing soft and low, thou tropic bird,
  From out the fragrant, flowery tree,
The ear that hears thee now has heard
  The ice-break of the winter sea.

Through his long watch of awful night,
  He saw the Bear in Northern skies;
Now to the Southern Cross of light
  He lifts in hope his weary eyes.

Prayers from the hearts that watched in fear,
  When the dark North no answer gave,
Rise, trembling, to the Father's ear,
  That still His love may help and save.

The following is of especial interest :—

THE WEDDING VEIL.

Dear Anna, when I brought her veil—
  Her white veil on her wedding night—
Threw o'er my thin brown hair its folds,
  And, laughing, turned me to the light.

"See, Bessie, see! you wear at last
  The bridal veil, foresworn for years!"
She saw my face – her laugh was hushed,
  Her happy eyes were filled with tears.

With kindly haste and trembling hand
  She drew away the gauzy mist:
"Forgive, dear heart!" her sweet voice said,
  Her loving lips my forehead kissed.

We passed from out the searching light—
  The summer night was calm and fair—
I did not see her pitying eyes,
  I felt her soft hand smooth my hair.

Her tender love unlocked my heart;
'Mid falling tears at last I said:
"Foresworn, indeed, to me that veil,
Because I only love the dead!"

She stood one moment statue-still,
And, musing, spoke in undertone:
"The living love may colder grow;
The dead is safe with God alone!"

The following poem to his sister was sent to her by Whittier, with a copy of his book, "The Supernaturalism of New England," which consisted of poems relating to the superstition and folk-lore prevalent in New England. It was written in 1847, and is full of early memories and tender thoughts:—

Dear sister! while the wise and sage
Turn coldly from my playful page,
And count it strange that ripened age
    Should stoop to boyhood's folly;
I know that thou wilt judge aright
Of all which makes the heart more light,
Or lends one star-gleam to the night
    Of clouded melancholy.

Away with weary cares and themes!
Swing wide the moonlit gate of dreams!
Leave free once more the land which teems.
    With wonders and romances!

Where thou, with clear discerning eyes,
Shalt rightly read the truth which lies
Beneath the quaintly-masking guise
    Of wild and wizard fancies.

Lo! once again our feet we set
On still green wood-paths, twilight wet,
By lonely brooks, whose waters fret
    The roots of spectral beeches;
Again the hearth fire glimmers o'er
Home's whitewashed wall and painted floor
And young eyes widening to the lore
    Of faëry folks and witches.

Dear heart! the legend is not vain
Which lights that holy hearth again,
And, calling back from care and pain,
    And death's funereal sadness,
Draws round its old familiar blaze
The clustering groups of happier days,
And lends to sober manhood's gaze
    A glimpse of childish gladness.

And, knowing how my life hath been
A weary work of tongue and pen,
A long, harsh strife with strong-willed men,
    Thou wilt not chide my turning
To con, at times, an idle rhyme,
To pluck a flower from childhood's clime,
Or listen at life's noonday chime,
    For the sweet bells of Morning!

EUGÉNIE DE GUÉRIN.

EUGÉNIE DE GUÉRIN.

We had the self-same world enlarged for each,
By loving difference of girl and boy.
—GEORGE ELIOT.

AMONG those who seem to have been born for ministry, and who have been distinguished by their capacity for tender devotion, few deserve to be more lastingly and lovingly remembered than Eugénie de Guérin, the honoured sister of Maurice de Guérin. Few instances of sisterhood are more deeply interesting and pathetic.

The Guérins are descended from an old and illustrious family of the Venetian race who were settled in France early in the ninth century, when one of the name (then spelt Guarini) was Count of Auvergne. One branch of the family became Lords of Montagu and Earls of Salisbury, who counted among their number Guérin, Bishop of Senlis.

Eugénie de Guérin was a member of the

branch who had for a long period been settled at Le Cayla, in Languedoc, in the sunny South of France, whose descent and nobility were fully recognised, but which had become very much impoverished during the troublous times of the Revolution. She was born in the year 1805, having a brother—Erembert, whose familiar name in the Le Cayla circle was Eran —a few years older. Next in order came Marie ("Mimi"); and when Eugénie was five years old, the youngest and most tenderly cherished—Maurice—was added to the little flock. Monsieur and Madame de Guérin were people of rare excellence, and they and their children were one and all bound by ties of the strongest affection, the example of loving self-denial set by their elders permeating the whole family.

Madame de Guérin was from the birth of Maurice in failing health; and in their earliest years the children, probably left much to themselves, were fond playmates, and learnt to love the dilapidated old château, which was their home, with its curious crannies and winding passages, no less than the solemn, whispering woods and smiling fields which surrounded it.

But Maurice was a delicate child, and had during his babyhood but a feeble hold upon life. His sister has said that "his soul seemed often on his lips, ready to flee away," and he lay ill for a year. The tenderness always shown by Eugénie to this brother thus began with his earliest years, and continued until his hard-fought life was closed. It was not her position as elder sister that dictated this so much as the lovingness of her sensitive nature, her disposition to protect and cherish all things weak and suffering. When Maurice was about two years old, Eugénie, who had been staying away from home, brought a little frock she had made for him. After she had dressed him in it she led him out of the house, and induced him to make his first few tottering steps. Then running to the house in excited delight, she gladdened her mother with the words: "Mother, Maurice has walked! has walked alone!"

From her childhood Eugénie was remarkable no less for her intelligence than for her religious sympathies. From the journal which she began to keep many years after we catch some pleasing glimpses of her childhood and home life. She was, as might be expected, brought up in the Roman Catholic faith; but in the Le Cayla circle the Catholic religion was one of sincere piety. We see in the Guérins the better side of Romanism, the good without a large admixture of the superstitions of that faith; and the only evil effect, if any, it had on the life of Eugénie was the encouragement of too much introspection, with its necessary accompaniment of a tendency to the morbid. She mentions that in saying her morning and evening prayers she was taught to kneel before a picture of the crucifixion. Here she brought her childish troubles before the representation of the dying Saviour and received consolation. On one occasion, having stained a new frock, she asked the Saviour to take away the stains in order that she might be saved a scolding. As the stains disappeared she believed her prayer had been answered. Believing, as she did, in the Divine presence always surrounding her, she imagined an angel given to have charge of the nursery, which she called the "Angel Joujou." Among the friends of her childhood she mentions a cousin Victor, who being a frequent visitor at Le Cayla, became a

great favourite, and helped very much to
smooth for Eugénie the difficulties of learning
to read, and then making her happy by wonderful stories and taking captive her warm and
loving little heart.

She became passionately fond of Nature,
both in its grander and more minute charms,
by day and by night. She has recorded how,
while on a visit to relatives at Gaillac, she
would after going to bed often get up, open the
window and lean out to watch the stars. As
this was carrying her love of Nature a little too
far, we cannot be surprised that, having one
night been discovered, her aunts took the pre-
caution of preventing her falling from the
window by having it nailed up.

So long as the childhood of the little De
Guérins lasted it was an intensely happy one.
But the time came all too soon when, for
Eugénie, the joys of childhood were to give
place to almost mature care; when her
childish affection for her brother Maurice was
to be succeeded by an anxious and almost
maternal solicitude. Madame de Guérin, for
years an uncomplaining sufferer, was taken
from them when Eugénie was thirteen,

Maurice eight. The impression left upon her mind by her mother's death was so great, and her grief so profound, that we find her after a lapse of sixteen years recording her feelings thus in her journal: "To-day my whole soul looks from the sky to a tomb, for on it sixteen years ago my mother died at midnight. This sad anniversary is consecrated to mourning and prayer. I have spent it before God in regrets and in hope; even while I weep, I lift my eyes and see the heavens where my mother is without doubt happy, for she suffered so much! Her illness was long, and her spirit patient. I do not remember a single complaint escaping her, or that she cried out at all, notwithstanding the pain that tore her; no Christian ever bore suffering better. One saw that she had learnt it before the Cross. She would smile upon her bed like a martyr on the rack. Her face never lost its serenity, and even in her agony she seemed to be thinking of a festival. This surprised me who saw her suffer so much, and I myself who wept at the least thing and knew not the meaning of resignation under pain. And when they told me that she was going to die I looked at her, and her cheerful aspect made me believe she would not. She did die, however, at midnight on April 2, whilst I had fallen asleep at the foot of her bed. Her quiet death did not waken me ; never did soul leave the world with more tranquillity . . . I was led into another room."

Before her death Madame de Guérin had committed the delicate little Maurice to Eugénie's protecting love. Henceforth she regarded him as a sacred trust, and while deeply loving all her kindred, while befriending all who came within the range of her sympathy, it was to Maurice her heart's great love went out with a yearning desire for his well-being. As years went on, and Maurice advanced in intelligence, all causes seemed to combine to draw the bond yet closer. There was not only the passionate sister's love, but hearts and mind were cast in a similar mould, and as tastes and inclinations became developed, the sacred promise to the dead mother—the tenderness of. heart which led Eugénie to care for all things feeble, were strengthened by the added charm of kindred thought and pursuit.

Eugénie has recorded that Maurice from his

earliest years showed a remarkable intelligence. One of his first masters on being asked by his father his opinion of his pupil replied, "Ah, sir! you have there a transcendant child." His sister said a pater every day that he might know his lessons. When only nine years old he was passionately fond of history and spent much leisure time with Rollin. He wept for joy at his first lesson in writing. She adds: "Maurice was an imaginative and dreamy child. He spent long periods contemplating the horizon. He was particularly fond of an almond-tree, under which he took refuge from any distraction. I have seen him remain there standing for whole hours." One of his enjoyments was to improvise sermons in the open air, which he declaimed, always with his sisters for audience, standing on a bank in the wood, which they called the pulpit of St. Chrysostom.

The delightful personal intercourse of the young brother came to an end for a considerable time, when at the age of eleven Maurice was sent to school at Toulouse. "Then commenced," says Eugénie, "between us that intimate correspondence that ended only with his death." Two fragments of his letters at that time she gives: "Dear Eugénie, I am much touched by the sorrow that you feel on account of my absence. I also regret you and I should wish much that it were possible to have a sister at the school. But do not disquiet yourself; I am very content here. My masters love me, my companions are excellent. . . . I am advancing with full sails into the Latin country. You shall have a better master at the vacations. Take care of my turtle-doves. I sing at the chapel. Adieu. I embrace you, and pray you to embrace my father and all the family. Tell them I am quite content to be here."

Again:

"Hélas, le monde entier sans toi.
    N'a rien qui m'attache à la vie."

"DEAR EUGÉNIE,—You will perhaps be astonished to see these two lines at the beginning of my letter. It is, so to speak, the text from which I wish to draw in order to better express the tender love that I bear you. The sentiment which inspired in Paul those words towards Virginia was not more sincere than mine. It is particularly to you that I give the Life of Voltaire. You will see there the genius and the perversity of that man, this coryphée of impiety, who put at the end of each letter : Let us crush the infamous thing, that is to say the Catholic religion. For me, I shall not cease to put there : 'I love you, I love you.' "

Both at Toulouse and at the College Stanislas at Paris, where he was removed a few years later, Maurice was remarkable for his ability and good conduct. " He attained the most brilliant success and formed distinguished and deep attachments."

During these school and college days Maurice was away from Le Cayla for five years, during which Eugénie passed from her seventeenth to her twenty-second year—the beautiful blossoming time of her life. Less dreamy and without the profound melancholy which became developed in her brother, and the fluctuations of spirit consequent thereon, she was contemplative, poetic, and decidedly religious. She delighted in committing her thoughts to paper. Nothing was too minute or insignificant for her felicitous description. The pleasure she derived from this occupation made her almost feel that it was of a character not to be encouraged. But she had also sweet household cares, which were never neglected, and loved the still repose of the country life where her lot was cast. Though not caring for society she had many friends and became a great correspondent, delighting those who received them with the charming and graceful style of her letters. It was about this time that she made the acquaintance of the most interesting family of Mons. de Bayne, who lived at Rayssac among the mountains, with one of whose daughters, Louise, she formed a close and lasting friendship.

A letter from Maurice to his sister, written from Paris, and dated October, 1828, shows so much of his inner life and of his feeling towards her that it should be given entire:—

" My Dear Eugénie,—Certainly much time has elapsed since I received any news from you or you from me ; I ought to confess that I am very culpable, and that upon me should rest the fault of the silence which ought never to exist between us. It is time at last to break it, and to repair our forgetfulness, or rather mine, by an assiduous correspondence which should place us in that intimate relationship which ought always to exist between a brother and a sister; that is to say, that we come near to each other, notwithstanding the distance which separates us, and make ourselves enjoy a conversation all the more sweet that distance throws a double interest on what we tell to the cherished object.

"My dear Eugénie, the lines which I am going to write will astonish you without doubt; the conduct which I have maintained towards you up to the present presaged nothing like what you are going to read, but be persuaded that I speak to you sincerely; your surprise, I believe, will be agreeable. Up to now I have shown you little confidence; but why, you will say? The reason of it is not in my heart; woe to me that there was ever the least *éloignement* for you! It is the fickleness of the age, it is this continual distraction, heritage of infancy, which follows us to that age where reflection takes the place of sports, and casts the first clouds on the face where there have shone, up to that time only, the candour of innocence and the expression of happiness. But here I am arrived at an age where childhood is for me only a dream; all the illusions of life have disappeared, and sad realities have taken their place. It is then that one is no longer sufficient for himself; it is then that the man who grows pale with dread, and who feels, so to speak, his knees to sink under him in view of the path of life, of that rough road where 'they climb rather than march'; it is then, say I, that man has need of a support, of a helpful arm which sustains him in the trials that he is about to undergo. This want manifested itself to me as soon as, casting a look upon the future, I saw myself alone ready to face so many dangers. Then my heart immediately fixed upon you; and can one indeed find a better friend than a sister such as you are? Be willing, then, henceforth to be a great deal my confidant, and help me with your advice and your friendship. But you will say, 'Ought you to have any other confidant than a father? Is it not he who ought to be the depository of all your secrets?' You may well believe that I have made this reflection; but papa is so sensitive, he is affected with so little a thing that I would never dare tell him all that passes within me. Then you are the one of all the family whose character is the most conformed to mine, so much I have been able to judge by your pieces of verse, all stamped with a sweet reverie, with a sensitiveness, with a tinge of melancholy in fine which makes, I believe, the foundation of my character.

"This expression, so far as I can judge of it, will have caused you some surprise; but this is what I wish to say: I was only fourteen years old when I quitted you—at that age one knows one's self, so to speak, only by sight—my reason was not sufficiently developed, nor capable of an examination sufficiently serious to lay hold upon the traits of your character. I do not believe that you were any more able well to know me, because I was too young to have a decided character. But how many changes have four years brought? What revulsions in this poor heart. People generally believe that I am light, frolicsome, playful, or, at least, such was the opinion that they had of me when I quitted the country; but my character has taken a turn quite different. I am able to say even that it is completely changed, and that there remains for me nothing of my childhood.

"But as the development of a character demands details which could not be given in this letter, I will make my following letters the subject of it. I will trace for you the history of my heart since the age when one begins to reflect to the present; I will make known to you my sensations, my reflections, and what habitually occupies my thoughts. I dare believe that these details will not be without interest for you; and I invite you to make me share also all that passes within you, if that does not weary you. For myself, it seems to me that we should be able to have a most interesting correspondence; for I believe that, in order to love one another, it is necessary perfectly to know each other; and I conceive no greater charm in life than that converse of two hearts who pour continually into each other all their secrets, all their feelings. We will converse also of literature, for it is the only thing, after friendship, which can make an agreeable diversion from the bustle and from the weariness of life; it is the only thing which can console us in our misfortunes and give vigour to our dejected soul. Give me books and plunge me in a dungeon, provided that I can there see clearly enough to read them, I should know how to console myself for the loss of my liberty. You will think, perhaps, that that is pushing the thing a little too far; but it is to make you feel that books can take the place of many things for him who knows how to love them."

Eugénie's fervent response to this appeal was such as to give entire satisfaction to the heart-yearning for her confidence and advice. She expresses a desire for arms long enough to embrace her brother wherever he might be, and he in turn assures her how much the inspiration of Nature, and her happy and facile genius, have endowed her, that she knows much more than he, with all his classica attainments.

In 1829 Mdlle. de Guérin was plunged into profound sorrow by the death of her most dear friend, her Cousin Victor. She grieved for him passionately for a long period. So lasting was the impression produced by this loss, that being reminded of the event by another death ten years later, she refers to it in her journal, in which she speaks of her cousin as a friend tenderly loved—the charm of her childhood.

Maurice finished his course at Stanislas without having formed any definite plan for his future life, and made a prolonged visit to Le Cayla in 1831. This was a happy interlude in their intense lives. Maurice was then about twenty-one, a child of much love and hope, and his home-coming was a time of rejoicing to all who had known him in his childhood.

It was now, however, necessary for him, as the younger son, to decide upon a profession as a means of livelihood, the somewhat impoverished acres at Le Cayla being considered only sufficient for his elder brother. The future of Maurice, became, therefore a matter of some anxiety in the Le Cayla circle; for although of decided genius and brilliant attainments, he showed a disposition to be desultory in his pursuits and tastes, and to lack the inclination and continuous application necessary for the regular study of the law, which his father desired him to follow. Meanwhile he enjoyed to the full the society of his sister, going to and fro among the old walks, confiding to her his aspirations and difficulties. With her he visited the cultured home of Mons. de Bayne, where he speedily became a great favourite, discussing with the father matters literary, social, and political, and forming a still more tender friendship with the charming daughter Louise.

But these days of sunshine could not last. Maurice was obliged to bid farewell to Rayssac, and to the sister to whom, during a few months, he had been drawn so much closer by this brief personal contact.

So in November, 1831, Maurice returned to Paris for the study of the law, this time taking up his abode with his cousin, M. Auguste Reynaud, and his wife, Félicité, in the Rue d'Anjou. How his sister's love followed him, and how she endeavoured to stimulate him in the studies and the perseverance necessary for his career, and to console him under his disappointments, we find from her letters. These letters, at the same time, give glimpses of life in the old home at Cayla, and also of the outer and inner life of Eugénie herself.

"*Cayla, November 9th*, 1831.

"How long is time when one is weary! Is it three years or three days since you went away, my dear Maurice? For me, I know nothing of it, for all that I know is that I am tired to death. Really, this is the only moment in which I have had any pleasure since you went; yet it will be very short. Jules is in haste to leave us for Paris. Thus, my dear, these few words will follow you without your having any expectation of them, as I have followed you sometimes quite softly to play you a trick. But, my God, how far away from us you are now! You ramble, are always rambling, further, and I follow you hardly knowing where I am going. I am afraid you will be upset, and I recommend you to the *petite croix*. I have great confidence that it will preserve you from all evil chance. Be devoted to it, as you have promised me, and I shall be tranquil. I am over head and ears in household affairs; but I have left them all to come to say a word to you in your little room, where I find strong reminders of you, without counting your vest and shoes. If you were dead these would be relics for me; but God preserve me from such a devotion.

"I shall go to Cahusac on Monday to see the fair and other things; the following Monday I expect to have news from you if you left Toulouse the day before yesterday. Nothing has happened since Sunday which is worth remembering. Rain, mud, wind, and to-day sunshine, that is all.

"I was forgetting a chicken that Wolf has killed, which cost him some blows with the whip which made him cry piteously. I believe that he called for you. The poor beast had reason for calling his wandering knight, for no one undertook his defence. Trilby kisses you, and licks your hands. For me, I hug you. Adieu.

"My influenza is leaving me, but it does not quit the house; the Shepherd has it yet, as well as Maritorne. People are dying of it at Franseilles; it is really to have death at one's heels. But have we it not always before, behind, and everywhere? Yesterday, at Andillac, a little child went to heaven. If I were a little child I should wish to follow him; but when one is old we never wish to die. It is because, then, all the little threads that bind us to the earth become cables. Papa sends you ten francs to subscribe for him to *The European Review*. I send you nothing but a couple of squeezes. I have not time to reply to-day to my cousin. Give her my love. Adieu."

"*Cayla, November* 24*th*, 1831.

"Here we are then again at our letters, my dear Maurice. It is not at all what I wish, but I content myself with it since I am not able to have you. A charming prophetess has just told me that I shall in a little time be consoled for your absence. If she believes that I shall forget you she is a false prophetess. Does she mean, then, that you will return? But this return is so far off! That you will write to me? That consoles me much, but not altogether. Behold, here it is! Yes; you will return to me; but it will be printed, gilded, bound. I see you an author, you rich in glory, and I in Paris. That is what she had wished to say; she knows that I wish it, this venerable little sorcerer, and she would not wish to announce misfortunes. I accept the augury, which, besides, your letter to me just confirms. You are at last launched in a career, far, very far, from that Code which weighed upon you like Mount Atlas. Papa is satisfied with your determination. . . . I was quite alone last week. Erembert was at Lacaze, and papa here and there, as you know he is with the fine weather. We have had a spring of four days. The evenings were delightful, but I did not go out to enjoy them all alone. I was then in my chamber, my elbows upon the window and my chin upon my hands; and I gazed, and thought, and regretted. Think of my being alone with Trilby, the only creature who comes to laugh with me. The little dog has had many caresses. Gazelle has also some desire to love me, but it comes and goes like a caprice. I like her, however, more than she knows for the good milk that she gives us.

"My thought often goes the round of the world in the twinkling of an eye. If my legs could follow it you know well where I would be. Truly I am often at the corner of your hearth, blowing and stirring the fire, and sending you a spark when you are too serious. I always imagine that your fireside nooks resemble our own a little, and that at the house of my cousin you find yourself at home again. At least, what you tell me of his wife makes me believe it. I am enchanted that we have so well divined. Tell me if that sweet figure has not that calm air that I think, a little in the style of Léontine.

"I have had a charming letter from . . . ; she speaks to me of Lucretia. That name, she says, will not go from her thought. When we are inclined to weariness Lucretia is there to bring back gaiety. I confess that in the place of M. M., I would rather get into raptures over a living person than a dead one, but that shows that he does not forget merit. Then she speaks of your future, and this after praises that you could not entertain better than those of the Abbé; that is why I do not tell you them. She adds: " He will be happy." Take that word as you would desire ; I leave you to think upon it, and especially to achieve it; for the being happy depends in part upon yourself. Not with that happiness which touches not the earth with its foot; but with that happiness of the manner of man, that little portion of felicity which God gives to him here below.

"There is a portion of your letter which has edified me much. It is well for us to say: Let us pray, let us pray. Yes, I have prayed, poor little ant that I am. I have prayed with very good heart for a happy voyage for our pilgrims. May God will that they return happy.

"I have not a single anecdote to tell you, only politics go always like spindles in the night studies of the hamlet. These women spin politics wonderfully. Poor Romiguires is taxed for ten francs—he or his asses. If every one in France pays as much, it will console the poor man. What would you wish that I should send to Rayssac? But you ought to write to M. de Bayne. Console the poor man; this news must have afflicted him. Mimi has written to me; she remains at Toulouse until the first of the year. I think that Jules has arrived safely. He must open his eyes very much in this great Paris. My influenza has left me: you will see this by this long letter. One of these days I shall write to my cousin. I should be much grieved if that correspondence falls asleep. It is said that the cholera is in England. I could wish it almost at Paris, in order to see you all three arrive here. Set out quickly if it approaches; tell my cousin so from me. But I hope to see you here under better auspices."

The pursuit chosen for Maurice by his father was distasteful to him, and from time to time he confides to his sister his struggles between duty and inclination—how much more he prefers history, religious philosophy, and poetry, and had hopes of a literary career Writing to her early in January he says:—
"From time to time discouragement, redoubtable discouragement, falls again on my soul like a weight of ice and paralyses all my courage and all my thirst for knowledge; but I struggle with all my strength; I call to my aid all that I have of hope and of ardour, and generally I raise myself up. These are, I assure you, terrible combats, profound shocks, these fits of dejection, these returns of the thought which becomes cold, gloomy, positive, desperate. It is a true malady of the soul."

Following this declaration of conflict and despondency we have a brighter picture: "My household life favours wonderfully my intellectual life. You know that I have a room, a very pretty room, where I have my bed, my fire, and my books; there I can work at my ease and in silence. I shut myself in this enclosure as in my empire, and, in fact, once the door is closed, the world is no more. I am alone with myself and my thoughts, with my poetry, my cherished books, and no one comes to trouble the secret of this sanctuary. Just now, for example, I am in one of my sweetest moments. It is half-past eight in the evening, it is cold outside, and a good fire burns in my chimney (the thought of the poor often spoils this pleasure for me), my little table is placed at the side, and I converse delightfully with you.

"When I do not pass my evening in my room, I pass it *en famille* with Auguste and Félicité. We talk as brothers and sister, or else we do some reading together. You see that my life sufficiently resembles that of Le Cayla, except all of you and the sweet face of the country, and the horizon which I loved to contemplate in the evening from the western corner of the terrace. It sets me longing when spring returns to give life to our little garden; the walk will not be so long as in our fields, but I shall always have verdure and the little path by the flowers. There is in the midst a great fir which is magnificent when it is covered with hoar frost; one should say, to see its overhanging and jagged branches—with grand silvered drapery." He then tells her that he has formed new friendships among the writers in *The European Review*, and that a contribution by him was accepted, and would appear in the next number. This review he asks her to send to Louise with an intimation that the essay was by him, and asks if she could obtain from her friend any indication of how he was regarded! Here is Eugénie's reply:—

January 22*nd*, 1832.

"It is Sunday to-day: the day for repose. So I hear no other sound than that which my pen makes on the paper. I am thinking of you. You are not so tranquil in your great Paris, except in your little chamber, where you find again Le Cayla in a more enjoyable form. When I saw yesterday the great oak of the Teoulet covered with hoar-frost, I thought of the great fir of Maurice. Nothing is more elegant than these trees in winter dress; but hurrah for their summer toilet! When one must only see trees, one loves better to have them green than white. For you, who see so many things, a little snow is nothing, and it is here a great event, especially when I used to make snowballs; but that has been for a long time a lost pleasure. Winter gives me only the sweet warmth of the chimney corner—that is the pleasure of the old. What a distance from the doll to the tongs! And there I am. And then will come spectacles, the cane, and the fall of the teeth—sad New Year's gifts! For at last the years make us all these presents. Since time brings me nothing sweet, I would willingly send back the first of the year as a tiresome creature who comes too often. As you say, It is strange that one is so gay at that period. That children are so very good, they catch bonbons; but we . . . Yet if I could have New Year's gifts sometimes according to my fancy. . . .

"I have, however, had one pleasing gift—your letter. Nothing gives me the pleasure of that. When I saw you more than ever wandering and straying in the land of the void, it is then that you show me that shut up in your room—confined to a regular work—what progress you have there made, my dear brother! Frankly, I did not expect so prompt a conversion. May God maintain it! I told you well that will is power. You have willed and have achieved; you have achieved even to the resumption of the code. I am quite content with you, and with your courage. Are you not well repaid for your first effort in seeing what it has produced? 'I now meet the day intrepidly.' It is the very thing for which you have made me wait so long, and it is that which makes me preach so much. Nothing gave me more pain than to see you so sick with life. You see how much sweeter she is when one knows how to lead her. It is for you the commencement of happiness to be able to think calmly. By little and little all will arrange itself, all will frame, all will harmonise in your existence. You will do like our old timepiece, which sounds very well when the weather is fine. Make it last, this fine weather that shines upon you now; and when the glacial discouragement shall come to fall upon you, fall again upon it as you have done already. He who gives one kick is able to give two, is able to give a thousand. I easily believe that these are terrible conflicts which these fits of dejection sometimes cause you. If I could cure you or help you. 'The Imitation' says something very true: '*Often the fire burns, but its flame rises not without smoke.*' It is very true; there arises not in us a good thought, a good intention, that is not quickly mingled with a little smoke, with a little human frailty. But the good God blows upon it, and it all departs.

"We have had some days of cold which makes the little birds cry. It is less sad than to hear the cry of the poor. I well believe that they spoil for you the pleasure of the fireside; but it pleases me to see that they cause you sorrow. If ever I come to knock at your door, I see that you will not close it against me. You would often hear rat-tat at your door if it were not so far off. For example, I would have come quickly to embrace you when I saw you so sage, so studious, so retired from the world. You have upon me the effect of a Father of the Church, studying the Bible and religious philosophy in your tranquil cell. I do not, however, think that any of them are as well lodged as you. But it is a charming abode! I can well understand that you make pretty verses within there, while stirring the fire. I feel sure that there are some everywhere in your room—upon the table, the chairs, at the corner of the fire; and I have nothing! Tell me, at any rate, what you are doing. Where is your drama? I should much love this Peter the Hermit. You would wish much, it seems to me, to present something to Lamartine. Do it, if you believe me. He will receive you, I am sure of it, as you would receive an angel, of whom you would ask encouragement and goodwill.

"I sent word to Rayssac, as you told me. There is no doubt that the Blessed Nicholas will be welcome. Who does not love the lives of the saints? I am not able to give you the explanations that you ask. How do you wish that I should set about it? It could only be in a *tête-à-tête* sometime that I should be able to ask it; in a letter never. Both the question and answer would be too indiscreet. In writing, content yourself, my dear, with the light and shade. Finally, Louise has not written since the long letter. I sent you in my last some lines with which you ought to be satisfied. Charles has made a great stir in the country, especially in the city of gossips; it was for this, it was for that, that he had to come to Cayla. They asked me what was his age, his fortune; and I heard it whispered, 'He is too young for her'; and she thought, 'What have you to bother yourselves about?' But they interfere with everything — from our wooden shoes to our consciences. They know everything — thoughts, words, acts, omissions, everything except how tiresome is their curiosity. I am for liberty of the press, but not for that of the tongue. They ought really to arrest some of those in this part of the country!

"Really you are leading the most charming life in the world. Our pastimes have but little resemblance to yours. One of these days, which was very cold, we went out, Mimi and I, to have a walk in the woods, and to pay a visit to the ravens; but, although well clothed, well muffled, the cold seized us. By good luck we found a fire of some young shepherds, who very graciously yielded to us the place of honour, a stone in front of the fire larger than the others. These children recounted to us all that they knew—one had just been eating some fry, the other had at home some fresh eggs laid by a red hen. From time to time they threw on the fire some handfuls of twigs, with an air of such content that there is no king who might not have said, 'Why am I not one of you?' If I knew how to make poetry I would sing 'The Shepherds' Fire.'"

The writing of articles for *The European Review* did not, however, form a means of livelihood for Maurice. He received no remuneration for them, and his endeavour to obtain more profitable employment failed. Having finally abandoned the study of the law, he returned home to Le Cayla in the spring of the year. The society of his beloved sister was not effectual to break the gloomy spell of his despondent thoughts. Though young and gifted, the melancholy natural to his peculiarly sensitive temperament was deepened by the result of his first struggle with his destiny; and he was unable to regard his future other than as one of failure and gloom. During this visit he began to write his journal, which became thenceforth, at intervals, a record of his struggles and hopes. It is a book of sweet sadness, containing at the same time many beautiful pictures of Nature, and thoughts of rare worth. The writing of journals at this time was probably an arrangement between Eugénie and her brother, as a mutual bond between them; for although that of the sister, which has been given to the world, was not commenced until two years later, it is only a continuation of a previous one which has not been found. In his perplexity the thoughts of Maurice now turned to the religious vocation, and he formed the project of joining a monastic institution at La Chênaie, conducted by Abbé de Lamennais. His father was reluctantly brought to give his consent, and, in the month of December, 1832, Maurice once more quitted Le Cayla, bidding another long farewell to his family for the solitude of La Chênaie.

It is not intended to trace the history of Maurice de Guérin except as it is associated with that of his sister. That it was so, however, to a great extent at every step, is indeed the fact. In so far as her yearning solicitude, her sisterly devotion, her almost maternal advice could make it so, they were never indeed apart. Her heart followed him, and when, during the succeeding year, he took, though with misgiving, the necessary vows initiatory to a religious vocation, she rejoiced at the promised fulfilment of her hopes concerning her beloved brother. But his subsequent course proved to be not in his own hands. The teaching of M. de Lamennais had become obnoxious to the authorities of the Church. The establishment was broken up. After being transferred for a time to a monastic institution at Ploërmel, the rigorous character of which was but ill suited to his fancy, an edict from the Bishop removing certain members, Maurice among the number, was welcomed by him as a release from toils under which his spirit chafed.

Upon leaving Ploërmel, Maurice did not return home, but after spending some time with friends at Mordreux, he set his face towards Paris, which was to be the scene of his future life. Here he, in the first place, turned his attention to literature, hoping to gain an entrance to the charmed circle of journalists. His experience only proved, however, to be that of many another young man both before and since. Not gifted with the dogged perseverance so essential in this pursuit above all, he found obstacles many and great, and the little remunerative employment he obtained not sufficient to keep the wolf from the door. After a struggle for a few months, an appeal was made to his father for assistance, while he was now looking about in the hope of obtaining work as a teacher. Two or three letters from his sister about this time show us that while absent from Le Cayla he was for ever present in her thoughts.

"*July* 15*th*, 1834.

"Two good letters have come to us, yours, my dear Maurice, and one from Felicité, who tells us of the situation offered you at Juilly. I hope you will not have said 'No,' unless it be for reasons unknown to us. What can present itself better, in your position, than a place where you will be able to see the future at no other cost than that of a little will and character. It is necessary to have a will for any one to be master in whatever circumstances. Thus one after the other all the faculties will be brought into play, and, the occasion having come, each will be ready for its work and will reply, 'Here I am.'

"I like what you tell me of the country, and the family life which you lead at the house of your friend. I remember that he wrote to you when you were here, and that he seemed to me to be quite devoted to you. He proves to us now how true it was. Tell him from me what pleasure the signal service rendered to you gives me, and the gratitude that I feel for his cordial affection. Has he a mother? Has he sisters? As I know that you are pleased to find us again anywhere, I ask if M. Vacher has sisters who fondle him, who pet brothers and chickens as we do at Cayla? Yesterday I saw one of my enjoyments die, one of these little pampered ones, devoured by a wicked stepmother. I covered it with sugar and with wine, but it is dead no less, and the poor little thing is now in the deep well, the great tomb of dead chickens and beasts. I have no stock this year but the poultry yard; neither birds' nests, nor sparrow. In caring for these little birds we are made to love them; but they die, and then one pities them. We have plenty of sorrows. Then it is also a loss of time. One finds it so precious that I become more and more greedy of it, and only with regret give a few minutes to pleasure. Really, I do not know what that is, for everything is changed into the useful for me, even the pleasure of writing to you.

"My correspondence always goes its pace. Long letters to the mountain, short ones to Gaillac, but often to Lisle as well. My beautiful Antoinnette cannot forget me, and sends me frequently pretty, gracious letters—charming heart-jewels. I owe her a reply, as well as others. Yesterday I had seven letters to write. My quiet room is a veritable post-office. You know how nice it is. At present I hear the grasshoppers singing, and from time to time a nightingale, who has his nest yonder among the juniper-trees. This side of Le Cayla is a little spoiled by the ruin of the great oak and the great cherry-tree, which were blown down in the winter; but this is nothing when we see the wood of Sept-Fonts all laid low—our dear walk without shade, our seats overturned, half broken; it makes me ill to see that, and I do not go there now, or I go only for reflection. Where shall I be?—where shall we be when these trees shall have become grown again? Others will go to walk under their shade, and will, like us, see winds which will make them fall. In all times there will be storms upon the earth.

"I am reading now 'Les Etudes de Chateaubriand.' After Lamartine, he is the poet I most love. Sometimes there comes to me a fancy to tell him so. Perhaps I shall do so, and I shall send it to you. I am working for my friend over there; and to cause her an agreeable surprise should like to make my piece fall under her eyes in the *Revue Europeanne* as by chance. Her father gets that journal, and Louise told me lately that she always looked for me there. M. Gazalé will not refuse you if the poetry of women is received in his journal. I am told it is, and I offer my flower. But let it be without name; I wish to be known only by Louise, who has no need that I name myself. Oh, that would give me pleasure! I am going to work at it, for it is not finished, then I will come again to tell you all papa wants you to know.

"There, that is done; my piece is finished; but not as I should like it; it wants something at the close, but I leave a blank, that I may not delay sending it to you. . . . Auguste ought to be happy with this little boy born to him. We had thought that you would be godfather. It is papa who here speaks, or rather makes me speak. . . . Adieu, my dear brother; I commend my poetry to you. If you are able to get it inserted, tell me; I will send it in manuscript. Eran is at Albi. Papa and Mimi embrace you, as I do, with all their heart.

"On the subject of poetry, I have had a thought for a long time which I wish to make you share. Have you not remarked that while we are inundated with so much poetry, there comes nothing for the children? Their little intelligence has, however, also its own wants, and their little heart its enjoyments. What pretty things there are to tell them! It seems to me, therefore, that a children's poetry is wanted by us, and would be welcomed. I have an inspiration : what think you of that? Is it necessary at last to get clear of my ideas by stifling them, or letting them go forth? I do not know why I have them; may God enlighten me. Reply to me on that subject, and tell me if I need fear loss of time, if my '*Enfantines*' would succeed. Then no more hesitation. I am at the work, otherwise I shall prefer making stockings to useless verses all my life. When we think of the account we shall have to render to God of all our actions, of all our moments, we have need to remember the use that we make of them. Life is so short to gain heaven, that each moment lost should be the occasion of tears.

"I have a sorrow of conscience or of heart. The priest is leaving the diocese—he of whom I have spoken to you. I regret him so much more, because he had given me permission to write to him, and I had hoped so much for that spiritual correspondence. Let us not speak of it. Do you remember me in your prayers? We ought to pray as much as to love. From me you have both the one and the other. Adieu."

"*September* 13*th*, 1834.

"Raymond departs in a month, and is to come to take our parcels for you, my dear

Maurice. I shall give him but little besides the little copy-book where I wish to write every day until your friend's departure. It will only be a letter of thirty pages, more or less, following events and the course of ideas, for sometimes many things happen in the mind and in the house, and at other times nothing at all!

"This week, for example, the habitual calm of Cayla has been broken by the arrival of our cousins from Thezac and Bellerive, who have come for the hunting. They are all quite big young men now, which makes one *think*, I who have seen them born .. . ."

"*September* 14*th*, 1834.

"It is Sunday : day for long walks at Cayla. So at sunrise Mimi and I were upon the heights of St. Pierre, going to the first mass at Cahusac. Now I am back, and thinking of the grand sermon of Father Bories. He is always our Massilon, speaking better than any other, and moralising marvellously. It is not his fault if those who hear him are not always very high in heavenly things. . . . Today I am well because I have taken the Communion. I remark with admiration the grand remedy which I find therein, and wherein, following the expression of St Francis de Sales, I feel I have the Saviour in the heart, in my head, in my spirit, and all my being. May this calm last with me! Then all is in health—the soul and the body; and poetry also comes to me again. It is only in times of peace that I sing. Do you understand that, my dear brother?"

"1834.

"An unexpected messenger passing at La Croix for Albi reminds me of our deputy, who, you have said, will willingly take charge of our letters. This will be short—an abridgement, a nothing, that I write at full speed in waiting for Delern, our messenger. It was papa who came quite out of breath from Pausadon to announce this departure to us, and behold pens in train, Mimi on one side and I on the other. She replies to your letter which came the day before yesterday, and I am only going to add a souvenir, after my courier of Friday. There is not much time, and as I should wish to write to Louise by the same means, that will make me rob you of a few minutes. You will not be sorry for it; and, besides, what should I say to-day that I have not said a hundred times? I say things over again. I repeat. I am like the old, repeating in the evening what they have said in the morning.

"But here is something fresh, a reproach; do not tremble, it is a complaint. I wish to tell you that your letter to Mimi would have given her much more pleasure if it had been longer, and if it had not failed to add a thousand things which are always wanting in your letters. Is it your fault or that of your masculine heart? Ours, it seems to me, understands better in friendship, and waits not to be asked for tenderness and all that one loves to see in a friendly correspondence. These poor brothers, we spoil them; we love them too much. We love them so warmly that to do the same seems impossible to them. But I wish to correct myself, and in place of the long epistles I have been accustomed to write you shall have only short ones. That is a resolution taken until you write to me according to my fancy. Adieu then to the little journal—of what use is it to me? You write to me no longer because of it. Nothing for nothing. I shall never know a word of your life because, say you, you would extend yourself so far on that subject I should grow weary in following you. Where would you then go, even though it should be to the end of the world, that I should not arrive with you? It is only a defect, an excuse for idleness, or for a heart a little frozen. You are going to be vexed, to complain. But why do you write so briefly? But for that letter to Mimi, I should say the most pretty things, or the most sweet at least, for I have not much bitterness in my soul, and already the sweet softness comes to me again. This poor Maurice, who without doubt loves us; what do I want from him, what am I demanding from him? Instead of thanking him for all that he does now, I am chiding him. That is not well. Then I am silent; let us embrace, and all is ended.

"How rich you are again, my brother, with your 1,800 francs! God be praised, and your friends blessed, and that good M. Buquet! Be well assured that papa forms no more rash judgments on them, and that we bear for them all the gratitude in the world for what they have done for you. Has your dear Lefebvre anything to do with your good fortune? I should like to know that he has. You know how I loved this friend of yours. And those of Brittany, shall we know no more of them? Answer me a word on their account, and do not forget La Chênaie if you know anything of it. Do you think that I have forgotten about it? Oh, no, but I never think of the fallen angel but with a feeling of the heart I am not able to express. Tell us what he is doing. For here it is said that he grumbles against Rome in his solitude, and that he has just published his "Philosophy." Our journals, however, have said nothing of it. It is true that it is only the poor little *Gazette du Languedoc*, that says nothing but gossip. Here is Delern. Adieu, my dear brother; I love you always. I have only time to assure Félicité and her family of all my affections."

The project mentioned by Mdlle. de Guérin of writing a book of children's poetry was not carried out. An over-sensitive and unhealthy conscience led her to believe that because she derived from the occupation great pleasure the desire should be discouraged. As a matter of self-sacrifice she abandoned the writing of poetry, whilst passionately loving it, and whilst she felt at the same time she was gaining power and inspiration, thinking it better for her soul's health to teach a word of catechism to little children than to write a volume of poetry. This must be regretted, as the few pieces which Mdlle. de Guérin composed of her proposed *Enfantines* are full of promise and of subtle charm. Writing on the subject she says: "There is no poetry for the children —poetry pure, fresh, laughing, celestial as their own souls, a poetry for their age. What is put into their hands is nearly always above their capacity, and is also not without danger, as the fables of La Fontaine. I would remove many of them from the collection for the first age, *to whom is due so much reverence.* Children are the angels of the earth. One ought to speak to them only in their language, to create for them only things pure, to paint for them in azure blue. Religion, history, nature offer rich pictures. But who will be the Raphael?"

As a specimen of the projected poems the

following may be given. As a little girl
Eugénie had imagined that an angel presided
over their play. This she called the Angel
Joujou, and afterwards put the idea into
verse :—

        L'ANGE JOUJOU.

    Il est des esprits puissants
    Qui dirigent les planètes,
    Qui font voler les tempêtes
    Et s'allumer les volcans,
    Qui règnent sur l'air et l'onde,
    Qui creusent le lit des mers,
    Qui règlent le cours du monde
    Et prennent soin des déserts,
    Qui sèment l'or et le sable,
    Lis et roses dans les champs ;
    Et dans le nombre innombrable
    De ces esprits bienfaisants,
    Il est un ange adorable
    Que Dieu fit pour les enfants,
    Un ange à l'aile vermeille,
    Une céleste merveille,
    Du Paradis le bijou,
    Le petit Ange Joujou,
    De l'ange gardien le frère ;
    Mais l'un guide l'âme aux cieux,
    Et l'autre enchante la terre
    Et ne préside qu'aux jeux.
    Il inventa la Poupée,
    Tant d'objets d'amusement
    Dont l'enfance est occupée,

Qui portent son nom charmant.
Avant l'aurore il se lève ;
Riant, il s'en vint du ciel
Dans l'Eden jouer près d'Eve
Avec le petit Abel.
Il fait les boutons de rose,
Les colliers de perle et d'or,
Les colibris qu'il dépose
Dans les fleurs du Labrador.
Il n'est merveilleuse chose
Qu'il n'ait faite ou fasse encor ;
Soufflant sur l'eau savonneuse,
Grâce à ses enchantements.
Brille un palais de diamants
A rendre une reine heureuse ;
Il fait le baume et le miel,
De son souffle nait la brise
Il a planté le cytiso
Et dessiné l'arc-en-ciel.
Passant du Gange en Norvége,
Il se mêle au beau cortége
Des cygnes éblouissants,
Et sème avec ses doigts blancs
Les jolis flocons de neige
Pour amuser les enfants.
Et ces concerts des campagnes,
Cette musique des bois,
Qui charment vals et montagnes,
De notre ange c'est la voix.
Ah ! que cet ange nous aime,
Et que ses pouvoirs son beaux !
Pouvoirs qu'il tient de Dieu même :
Il veille au nid des oiseaux ;
Il leur porte du ciel même

> Leur vêtement radieux
> Et deux perles pour leurs yeux.
> Il est de toutes nos fêtes ;
> Il tient pour nous toujours prêtes
> Des coupes sans aucun fiel,
> Et grâce enfin à ses charmes,
> On dit que toutes nos larmes
> Ne sont que gouttes de miel.
> Puis quand les dernières heures
> Sonnent aux pieux enfants,
> On le retrouve aux demeures
> Où sont les saint Innocents,
> Jouant avec leur couronne
> Et leur palme de martyrs,
> Bénissant Dieu, qui leur donne
> Tout le ciel pour leurs plaisirs.

After much hope deferred and sickness of heart, Maurice, towards the end of 1834, received a permanent engagement at Stanislas. It was by no means a lucrative one, but it sufficed to save him from the much-dreaded dependence upon others. In November of this year Eugénie began to write her journal, since famous, "A mon bien-aimé frère Maurice." This she designed to forward to him at intervals as an encouragement and solace, to remind him of ties still existing in the beloved home of his boyhood.

A few extracts from this journal will serve

to show the graceful style of Mdlle. de Guérin as a writer, her keen power of observation, her ability to find enjoyment and food for reflection in the most trifling things:—

"*November 15th*, 1834.

"Since you wish it, my dear brother, I am about to continue this little journal, which you like so much. But as I want paper I serve myself with a stitched copy-book designed for poetry, of which I am taking out only the title; thread and leaves all remain there, and you shall have it, bulky as it is, on the first opportunity.

17th.—" Three letters since yesterday—three very great pleasures, for I love letters so much, and those who write these, that is Louise, Mimi, and Félicité. This dear Mimi tells me charming and sweet things about our separation, about her return, her *ennui*, for she is wearied so far from me as I am wearied without her. Every moment I see I feel that she wants me, especially at night, when I am accustomed to hear her breathe into my ear. This little sound makes me sleep. Not to hear it makes me think sadly. I think of death, which makes such silence all around us; also an absence. These thoughts of the night come and mingle with those of the day. What maladies they speak of, what deaths! The clock of Andillac has sounded only knells these days. It is the malignant fever which makes its ravages every year. We are all mourning a young woman of your age, the most beautiful, the most virtuous of the parish, carried off some days ago. She left an infant at the breast; poor little one! It was Marianne de Gillard. Last Sunday I went again to press the hand of one at the point of death eighteen years old. She recognised me, the poor young girl, said a word to me, and resumed her prayer. I wished to speak to her, but knew not what to say; the dying speak better than we. She was buried on Monday. What reflections to make on these fresh tombs. O my God, how quickly people depart from this world! In the evening, when I am alone, all these forms of the dead visit me again. I have no fear, but my thoughts are all mournful, and the world seems to me as sad as a tomb. I have said, however, that these letters have given me pleasure. Oh!

it is very true; my heart is not mute in the midst of these agonies, and feels only more keenly what life brings it. Your letter, then, has given me a gleam of joy—nay, a veritable happiness—by the good things with which it is filled. At length your future begins to dawn; I see for you a calling, a social position, a point of support in real life. God be praised! It is what I desired the most in the world for you and me, for my future is joined to yours; they are brothers. I have had beautiful dreams on this subject; I will, perhaps, tell you them. For the moment, adieu; I must write to Mimi.

"18*th*.—I am furious with the grey cat. This naughty animal has just carried off a little pigeon that I was trying to re-animate by the corner of the fire. It was beginning to revive, poor creature! I wanted to tame it—it would have loved me; and, behold! all the fond hope scraunched by a cat. How many are the disappointments of life! This event, and all those of the day, have happened in the kitchen. I remain there all the morning and a part of the evening while I am without Mimi. It is necessary to look after the cook. Papa sometimes comes down, and I read to him by the oven, or the corner of the fire, some pieces from 'The Antiquities of the Anglo-Saxon Church.' This great book astonished Pierril. 'What words there are there!' he exclaimed. This child is quite droll. One evening he asked me if the soul was immortal; afterwards what was a philosopher. We were on great questions, as you see. Upon my replying that a philosopher was a person wise and learned, 'Then, mademoiselle,' said he, 'you are a philosopher.' This was said with an air of *naïveté* and of freshness which might have flattered Socrates, but which made me laugh so much that my gravity as catechist went for the night. This child has left us lately, to his great regret; the term was up on St. Brice's day. Now he goes with a little pig seeking truffles. If he comes by here I shall ask him if he sees in me yet a philosophic look.

"With whom do you think I spent this morning by the corner of the kitchen fire? With Plato. I durst not say it, but he came under my notice, and I wanted to make his acquaintance. I am only at the earliest pages. He seems to me to be admirable, this Plato;

but I find in him a singular idea. He places health before beauty in the list of the good things which God gives us. If he had consulted a woman Plato would not have written that! Do you think it good? Remembering that *I am a philosopher*, I am rather of his opinion. When one is very ill in bed, one would willingly sacrifice complexion or beautiful eyes in order to recover health and enjoy sunshine. When I was a child I should have wished to be beautiful; I dreamed only of beauty, because I said to myself, Mamma would love me more. Thanks to God, that age of infancy has passed, and I enjoy no other beauty than that of the soul. Perhaps even in that I am a child, as formerly: I should wish to resemble the angels. That also might be displeasing to God, for it is also that one might be loved more. What things come to me if it were not necessary to leave you! But my chaplet, I must say it. The night has come; I like to finish the day in prayer.

"20*th*.—I love the snow. This white expanse is something celestial. The mire, the naked earth displeases me, saddens me; to-day I perceive only the trace of the roads and the footmarks of the little birds. Softly as they alight, they leave their little traces, which make a thousand figures upon the snow. It is pretty to see the little red claws, which as crayons of coral design them. The winter has its beautiful things, its adorning. We find charms everywhere when we learn to see them. *God sheds grace and beauty everywhere.* I must now go to see what there is pleasant at the corner of the kitchen-fire; sparks if I wish. This is only a little goodmorning I am saying to the snow and to you on jumping out of bed.

"It has been necessary to prepare an extra dish for Sauveur Roquier, who has come to see us. It was ham, cured in sugar, over which the poor boy licked his lips. Good things do not often come to his mouth; it is therefore that I wish to treat him well. It seems to me that it is to the destitute we should give attention—humanity, charity tell us so.

"No reading to-day. I have made a hood for a little one, which has taken all my time. But provided one works, whether it be with the head or the fingers, it is quite equal in the eyes of God, who takes account of every work done in His name. I hope, then, that my hood will take the place of a charity. I have given my time, together with a little skin from my fingers which the needle has taken off, as well as a thousand interesting lines that I should have *been* able to read. The day before yesterday papa brought me from Clairac 'Ivanhoe' and 'The Age of Louis XIV.' Here is provision for some of the long winter evenings.

"It is I who am the reader, but by fits and starts. It is sometimes a key that is wanted, a thousand things, often myself, and the book is closed for a moment. Ah! Mimin, when will you return to help the poor housekeeper, by whom you are wanted every moment? Have I told you that yesterday I had news of her at the market of C——, where I went? What yawns I left upon that poor balcony! At last the letter of Mimi arrived, quite on purpose to relieve my weariness, and it was the only pleasant thing I saw at C——.

"I put nothing here yesterday; a blank page is better than trivialities, and I should not have been able to say anything else. I was tired, I was sleepy. To-day it is much better; I have seen the snow come and go. Since I got my dinner a fine sun has shone; no more snow; at present the black, the ugly reappear. What shall I see to-morrow morning? Who knows? The face of the world changes so quickly!"

24*th.*—" How beautiful must be the heaven of heavens! This is what I have been thinking during the time I have just spent in contemplation under a most beautiful winter sky. It is my practice to open my window before going to bed to see what sort of weather it is, and, if fine, to enjoy it a moment. To-night I looked longer than usual; it was so ravishing, this beautiful night. But for the fear of taking cold I should be there still. I thought of God, who has made our prison so radiant; I thought of the saints, who have all these beauteous stars beneath their feet; I thought of you, who were, perhaps, looking up to them like me. I could have stayed there easily all night; however, it was necessary to shut the window to all the beauty outside, and to close the eyes under curtains. Eran has brought me to-night two letters from Louise. They are charming, ravishing to the mind, soul, and heart, and all for me. I know not why I am not transported, intoxicated with friendship. God knows, however, that I love it!

"No place in the world is so pleasant to me as home. Oh! the happy home! How I grieve for you, poor exile, so far from it, seeing only your kindred in thought, being unable to bid good morning or good night, living a stranger, having father, brother, sisters, not living with you but elsewhere! All that is sad, but I cannot desire anything else for you. We cannot have you, but I hope to see you again, and that consoles me; a thousand times I think of that, and foresee how happy we shall be."

29*th*.— . . . "Oh! how sweet it is, when the rain is heard pattering, to be by the corner of one's fire, tongs in one's hand, making sparks! This was my amusement just now. I am very fond of it; sparks are so pretty! They are the flowers of the chimney. Really, there are charming things going on about the embers, and, when I am not occupied, I amuse myself in watching the phantasmagoria of the hearth. There are a thousand little hearth-forms coming, going, dilating, changing, disappearing; now angels, now horned demons, children, old women, butterflies, dogs, sparrows. One sees a little of everything in the firebrand. I remember one figure, bearing an expression of heavenly suffering, which seemed to me to depict a soul in purgatory. I was struck by it, and should like to have had a painter with me. There was never a vision more perfect. Notice the logs burning and you will agree with me that there are beautiful things, and that unless we are blind we ought not to find time tedious beside a fire. Listen especially to that little whistle which sometimes comes from below the burning coal, like a voice that sings, Nothing is more sweet or pure; one would say it was some very diminutive spirit of fire that sings."

Last day of December.—" Christmas is come; beautiful festival, the one that I love the most of all, which brings me as much joy as to the shepherds of Bethlehem. Truly, the whole soul sings at this glad advent of God, which is announced on all sides by carols and the pretty nadalet. In Paris nothing can give you the idea of what Christmas is. You have not even the midnight mass. We all went to it, with papa at our head, by an enchanting night.

Never was there a more beautiful sky than that midnight one, so that papa from time to time put his head from under his cloak to look up. The ground was white with hoar-frost, but we were not cold; the air, besides, was warmed before us by the torches that our servants took to light us. It was charming, I assure you, and I wished I could have seen you walking along, like us, towards the church, through roads bordered with little bushes, white, as if in full blossom. The frost makes beautiful flowers. We saw one sprig so pretty that we wanted to make a nosegay of it for the blessed sacrament, but it melted in our hands. All flowers are short-lived. I much regret my bouquet; it was sad to see it melt and disappear drop by drop. . . . Here then are my last thoughts, for I shall write nothing more this year. In some hours it will be finished; we shall begin another. Oh! how fast time flies! Alas! Alas! Would one not say that I am regretting it? My God, no; I regret neither time, nor what it takes away from us. It is not worth while to throw one's affections into the torrent. But the empty, careless days, lost as regards heaven, these are what cause regret and make us think upon life. Dear brother, where shall I be on this same day, at this same time, this instant, next year? Shall I be here or elsewhere? Here below, or above? God knows; and here I am at the gate of the future, resigning myself to whatever can issue from it. To-morrow I shall pray that you may be happy; for papa, for Mimi, for all whom I love. It is the day of gifts. I am going to take mine to heaven. I draw everything from thence; for, truly, on earth I find but few things to my taste. The longer I live here, the less I enjoy it; and accordingly I see, without any regret, the approach of years, which are so many steps towards the other world. It is neither pain nor sorrow which makes one think thus, do not suppose it. I should tell you if it were; it is the home-sickness which takes hold of every soul that sets itself to thinking of heaven. The hour strikes, the last that I shall hear while writing to you. I would have it without end, like all that gives pleasure. How many hours have been marked by that old clock, that dear piece of furniture that has seen so many of us pass, without ever going away, like a kind of eternity! I am fond of it, because it has sounded all the hours of my life, the most beautiful when I did not listen to them. I can remember that my crib stood at its foot, and I used to amuse myself by watching the hands move. Time amuses us then; I was four years old. . . . My lamp is going out; I leave you. Thus ends my year, beside a dying lamp."

"The little Morvonnais, her mother tells me, sends me a kiss. What shall I give her in return for a thing so pure, so sweet as a child's kiss? It seems to me as if a lily had touched my cheek."

> Glad would I run, my child, at thy soft call,
>   Saying: "I love thee, I would like to kiss thee;"
> And when thy little arms, like two white wings,
>   Thou openest wide to embrace me!
>
> I have white lambs that often me caress,
>   A dove as well lays on my lips its beak;
> But when a child doth give me soft embrace,
>   'Tis as a lily rested on my cheek;
>
> Filling with balmy innocence my face,
>   And making all my life more pure and mild;
> Pleasure ineffable, celestial grace!
>   Who would not have thy kisses, blue-eyed child?

"A daughter ought to be so sweet a thing to

her father! We should be to them almost as the angels are to God. Between brothers it is different; here there is less consideration and more freedom."

Under date May 13, 1837, she writes:—"A sorrow. We have got Trilby poorly—so ill that the poor beast will die. I was fond of my pretty little dog. I remember, too, that you used to be fond of her and to caress her, calling her *little rogue*. All kinds of memories attach themselves to Trilbette, and make me regret her. Small and great affections—everything leaves us and dies in its turn. The heart is like a tree surrounded with dead leaves. . . .

"I have just had a young pigeon brought to me, which I am going to keep, and tame, and caress. It will replace Trilby. This poor heart always wants something to love; when it loses one object it takes another. I notice this, and that we keep loving without interruption, which shows our destination to eternal love. Nothing helps me better to understand heaven than to picture it to myself as the place of love; for if even here we cannot love for a moment without happiness, what will it be to love for ever?"

Maurice was, meanwhile, stung with the feeling that his life was a failure. He, indeed, resigned himself with a sense of hopeless indifference to his lot. It was in bitterness of soul, if with conscientious purpose, that he continued the monotonous, and to him uncongenial, task of teaching, when the bright dream of his youth had been so different—of poetry and literature, with his helpful sister Eugénie, if not a still dearer one, by his side. How different the stern reality! He reproached himself for his want of success. Entries in his journal at this time show the agony of soul of this sensitive plant, destined to live in the world's stony places. Here is one of June, 1835 :—

"What makes me at times despair of myself is the intensity of my suffering for little things and the for-ever-blind and aimless purposes to which I put my moral powers. To stir a grain of sand I use energy that might suffice to force a stone up to the mountain-tops. I could better bear the heaviest burdens than this light, almost impalpable, dust that clings to me. I perish secretly day by day. Life escapes me by invisible stings. I am weary of what surrounds me. I know neither where I would live nor in what profession; but I detest mine, which is spoiling me and making me wretched. It upsets at every instant the little philosophy that I can glean in free and tranquil hours, and vexes me with men still children. How I hate myself in these miseries! How I long to spring upon some shore of liberty, pushing back with my foot the odious bark which has carried me."

During all this trying period the love of Eugénie for her brother did not wane, nor did her confidence in him, in his genius and ultimate success, become abated. Troubled as she herself was with mental conflicts, with a constitutional melancholy which made her peculiarly sensitive to the pangs of bereavement, to the sorrows of all around her, and all the weariness of daily life, she never forgot her brother. Her journal, written as it was to him, discloses a life of the most tender solicitude and most pathetic interest on the part of a sister towards a brother on record. She poured out to him her heart's most inmost feelings. If his correspondence flagged, she became anxious, and, as it has been seen, tenderly expostulated, lovingly upbraided, gently warned. A new source of anxiety to her at this time was what she conceived to be a growing indifference on the part of her brother to religion. It appears that Maurice had for a time lost the devotion of his youth. His brooding melancholy and want of success had so far embittered his spirit that a cold and cynical philosophy was fast taking the place of his early faith and love. His long silences troubled his sister, and she braced herself to helpful and loving counsel. Opening her journal almost at hazard, we find such entries as the following:—"When every one is occupied and I am not needed, I retreat early and come here to write, read, or pray. I put here both what passes in my soul and in the house, and in that way we shall find day by day all the past. For me it is nothing, and I would not write it, but I say to myself, 'Maurice will be very glad to see what we are doing whilst he is far away, and thus enter into the family life,' and I mark it for you."

Again, she writes: "I have just passed the night writing to you. The day has replaced the candle, so that it is hardly worth while to go to bed. Oh! if papa knew it! How quickly it has passed, my brother, this night spent in writing to you! The dawn appeared whilst I believed it midnight; it was past three o'clock, and I had seen many stars pass, for from my table I see the sky, and from time to time I look at it and consult it; and it seems to me that an angel dictates to me. From whence, except from above, can come to me so many things tender, ennobling, sweet, true, pure, with which my heart is filled as I speak to you? Yes, God gives me them, and I send them to you. May my letter do you good. It will come on Tuesday. I have written it to-night so that I can give it to the postman in the morning and save a day. I was so drawn to come to you to divert and strengthen you in the state of feebleness and weariness in which I see you. But I do not see it; I divine it after your letters, and some words of Felicité. Would to God I could see and know what torments you, then I should know where to apply the balm, whilst I now place it by chance. Oh! how I long for letters from you! Write to me; speak, explain, show yourself, that I may know what you suffer. Sometimes I think it is only a little of that black melancholy which we are both liable to, and which makes us so sad when it spreads in the heart."

The apparent indifference of her brother sometimes, indeed, caused Eugénie to neglect her journal and her correspondence. He endeavoured to bear his troubles as he did his poverty, in silence; and when he was unable for want of the necessary means to travel, to spend his vacations at Le Cayla, the real cause was unknown, and was not unnaturally attributed to a waning affection. A letter from Eugénie, after a visit to Rayssac, where she had last been with him four years before, contains some charming pictures:—

"*September* 6*th*, 1836.

"It is a week since I came down from the mountains, quite sad, thinking of Louise, my heart full of our friendship, and with regrets for our separation. What it costs to go away from a friend, when we have found so much happiness together! To say adieu is a word that makes us weep, which kills. Fenelon is quite right in saying that friendship which makes much happiness for life, gives also inexpressible pain. We felt this, Louise and I. It is from their depth that the sweetest things of life have their bitterness. I learn it, I feel it continually more. What is to be done about it? To resign oneself, to habituate oneself to the course of the world which passes so changingly.

"My brother, I have thought of you everywhere among the mountains, under the linden trees, in the little salon, in the gallery, where they have made me read from your letters, those dear letters which M. de Bayne preserves with other precious papers. I believe you would give him much pleasure in sending him others from time to time, telling him now and then what passes in the literary world. This brave man especially loves you. The name 'M. Maurice' ought to be in his heart, for he has it often upon his lips. This affection ought to please you; I take pleasure in it, inasmuch as it apparently confers something upon me as your sister. In short, I know not why Mons. de Bayne treats me in so distintinguished a manner. He used to come and talk with me of his great authors, of his great thoughts; we conversed about all kinds of books—history, philosophy, legends, poetry.

That was a course of literary conversations for the evening, for it was in the evening that we talked, he in his armchair, the back to the window, I upon the large sofa, in the place marked by the countess; Leontine at the end, Louise upon a chair near me, and Criquet at her feet or on her lap. You should have seen also the round table with books, pamphlets, journals, stockings heaped up round the chandelier and below the shadow where the cricket used to come. It was the same as it was four years ago, except that you were not there. Louise is not at all changed. She has the same air of youth, the same gaiety, the same eye of fire. What a glance! I could wish that it had fallen upon Raphael. For myself, I have in my soul a charming tableau of it and a true one.

"I was cut off from it all at once by the arrival of Miou, my scholar, a little girl, sweet, pretty, and foolish according to papa, who does not like her slowness, which makes him judge sharply my poor *protégé*. A hail came the day before yesterday to carry off our grapes. It is a pity to see the poor bruised vines which promised an abundant harvest. They expected no less than seventy casks ; rely upon nothing in this world !

"To-morrow we expect the Reynauds, great and small. Papa longs infinitely to embrace Auguste, his wife, and the children. I had this pleasure the first, on my way to Albi. Judge of the happiness, and how the friendship of Felicité was soon formed. The appearance of friends that we had at first sight surprised every one—those who knew not that we already knew each other in heart. I found our cousin good, simple, friendly, loving you much, which makes me love her not a little. We talked of you: Tell me about Maurice; what is he doing? Does he think about us? When will he at length come? I have many other questions to ask her, which I will do one of these days when I have more leisure. It rains, unfortunately, which will prevent our going out, and sitting under some oak tree, where it is good to tell our secrets.

"If we had you also, what happiness! Let us not think of it, since thinking of it only brings us more regrets. However, you remember that I wish for you, that we wish for you, next year. Arrange accordingly, or tell us that you do not wish to come. I see nothing that can detain you; but from now you have a year to prepare. Prepare, or rather present yourself without hesitation. A little courage, come; the courageous prevail. Think of the pleasure you will do us, of that you will give to papa, the dear father who loves you so much that we should be jealous, if we had not also our share of tenderness. The heart of a father is infinite."

But shortly a still further source of anxiety as to Maurice began to afflict the Le Cayla circle. His constitution, never strong, had been very much undermined by the privations and hardships he had undergone. He was compelled for a time to give up his duties; and after struggling through the winter to resort to his native air, spending a considerable part of the year—1837—once more in the dear old home. Here confidences were completely restored, and after a time the sweet change and the loving care of his sisters brought about a more favourable condition, and Maurice's health seemed reassured.

His life had also recently received another stimulating motive. Maurice had never been without friends, and the entrée into good Parisian society, where his distinguished, if pensive, appearance, engaging manners, and powers of conversation had made him a favourite. Here he had made the acquaintance of a young orphan lady, of good family and fortune, called Caroline de Gervain, who lived under the guardianship of an aunt. A mutual attachment sprang up between them, and the autumn of this year was enlivened for Le Cayla by a visit from Mdlle. de Gervain and her guardian.

Upon her brother's partial restoration to health, the chief care of Eugénie in regard to him was his disregard of all religious duties. On the day of his return to Paris, in January, 1838, she writes in her journal: "I enter again for the first time this room where you were only this morning. Oh, how sad is the chamber of an absent one! We see tokens of you everywhere, but find no part of the real person. Here are your shoes under the bed, the table quite filled, the mirror suspended from the nail, the books which you read yesterday evening before going to sleep, and I who kissed you, touched you, looked at you!

What is this world where everthing disappears? Maurice, my dear Maurice, oh!

"When you had gone I went to church, where I could pray and weep at my ease. What do you do, who never pray, when you are sorrowful, when your heart is bruised? For me, I feel that I have need of a consolation more than human, that it is necessary to have God for a friend."

On learning of his arrival she writes (February 8): "Oh! letters; .letters from Paris, one of yours! You arrived well, happy, and welcome. God be praised! I have that only in my heart. I say to everybody, 'Maurice has written to us: he has finished his journey safely, had fine weather,' and a hundred things which come to me. A beautiful day, fine weather, sweet air, the clear sky. We only need to see the leaves to believe that it is the month of May. This radiant nature soothes the spirit, disposes it for some happiness. It was impossible, I thought, in my walk this morning, that something was not going to happen, and I have your letter. I did not deceive myself. These letters, this writing, what pleasure it gives!

How the heart fastens there and is sustained. But after a while one becomes sad again, the joy falls, regret rekindles and finds that a letter is only a little thing in the place of some person. We are never satisfied; all our joys are mutilated. God wills it, God wills it thus that the better part of us which yearns shall only be satisfied in heaven. There shall be happiness in its fulness, there the eternal reunion."

Again she writes:—

"A letter from Caroline. What happiness to know you are so much loved, so cared for . . . God be praised. I am tranquil. I see in all this a providential arrangement which makes everything for your good. And then you do not love the good God. His cares for you shine to my eyes like diamonds. See, my brother, all that comes to solace your poor position, these unhoped-for succours, this family affection, this mother, this sister, more than sister, so loving, so sweet, so beautiful, who promises you so much happiness. Do you not see something there, some Divine hand that orders your life? At present I hope for you a future better than the past—that past which has caused us so much suffering. But we all have our time of trouble, misfortune, servitude in Egypt, before the manna and the calm."

Again :—" Is the world in which you move rich enough for your needs ? Maurice, if I could make you enter into some of my thoughts thereon, to show you what I believe and what I learn from devotional books, those beautiful reflections of the Gospel! If I could see you a Christian I would give life and everything for that."

After returning to Paris Maurice suffered a sharp relapse, upon his partial recovery from which his marriage was fixed to take place in November. Eugénie was to go to Paris to be present. Before departing she went to Rayssac to spend a few days with her dear friend, Louise de Bayne, who had recently lost her father. A few tender words in her journal upon saying farewell show that her character as a friend was no less true than as a sister: " At seven o'clock I embraced her, and left her all in tears. What affection there was in her good-bye, that pressure of the hand, the '*Come again!*' the utterance choked by tears! Poor, dear Louise, I have had the courage to leave her and not to weep at all. . . . But what matter? I love as much as another; what comes from the heart is worth as much as what flows from the eyes. But this tender Louise loves and weeps. It is because she is very sorry to lose me; she has need of a friend. She told me her trials, her plans, her prospects, perhaps her illusions. Women always have some illusion."

The journey to Paris and a stay there of some months was quite an event in the quite life of Mdlle. de Guérin. On September 29, she writes in her journal: "Adieu, my little room; adieu my Cayla; adieu my copybook, which I will take with me, but it will go in my trunk." In the interval between this time and the following month of April the journal was, however, discontinued, or has not been found. From letters written during this period to her father and friends, we have pleasing glimpses of her life in Paris. During her visit there, as the guest of the aunt of Mdlle. de Gervain, she was welcomed by the best society, and spent much time in visiting the many places of interest, and making the acquaintance of an hitherto unknown world. Her one source of anxiety was the continued enfeebled condition of her brother's health. Writing to her friend Louise, she says, alluding to this: " When I am with others I imitate their liveliness, but at church and alone I have my own thoughts. I have everything I could wish for; they all love me here; I ought to be happy, but I am weary in spirit, and I say to myself that happiness is nowhere in this world."

The wedding was duly celebrated with much rejoicing and gaiety, and Eugénie wrote a charming account of it to her father, giving all details, as only a woman can, and declaring that all had passed as happily as at the marriage of Cana. She speaks in terms of loving praise of Maurice's " angel of a wife," and does not forget to say that upon the marriage morn Caro read to her husband a chapter of the *Imitation*.

The interval between December and the succeeding July was spent by Eugénie partly at Paris with her brother, and partly in visiting friends at Nevers and other places. She was deeply solicitous for her brother and his young wife. This was not without cause, for the young bride had married a dying man.

During her stay at Nevers, in April, she recommences her journal to her brother, which he was never to read:—

"Is it eight days, eight months, eight years, eight ages? I know not how long, but it seems endless in my weariness since I left you, my brother, my poor invalid. Is it well with you? Is it better? Is it worse? . . . . What painful ignorance, and how difficult to bear, this ignorance of heart, the only thing which makes us suffer, or which makes us suffer more. It is beautiful weather. One feels everywhere the sun and the presence of flowers, which would do you good. Springtime warmth would be more curative for you than any medicine. I say this in hope, alone in my hermit's chamber, with a chair, cross, and little table, under a little window where I write. From time to time I look at the sky and hear the bells and the passers-by in the streets of Nevers, the sad. Does Paris spoil me, make me gloomy anywhere else? Never was there a city more desolate, dark, and wearying, notwithstanding the *charmes* that inhabit it, Marie and her amiable family. I have tried everything, even drawing my distaff from its case where it has been since my departure from Le Cayla. It recalled to me the story of the shepherd, who, arriving at the Court, kept there the chest containing his crook, and sometimes found pleasure in opening it. I have also found pleasure in again seeing my distaff and spinning a little. But I spun so many things besides!"

Here, also, she received from her brother his last letter:—

"*April* 8*th*, 1839.

"Rain and cold must have accompanied you all the journey, my dear friend; they tell me that every day the weather has been horrid. But, at the time of writing, I have the consolation of thinking that for two days you have enjoyed rest after fatigue. In that assurance my thought has left the road to Nevers to follow that for Toulouse, where Eran is going, always with the same cortége ' of wind, of cold, and of rain.' Poor Eran! He left me with an emotion that touched me very much. This journey to Paris, and all that has happened in a few months, has drawn together and mingled

our lives (Eran's and mine) more than twenty years had been able to do. We have always lived far away from each other, and our characters have not helped much to make up for distance. At length, events have hastened what must happen sooner or later, at our age, and we parted with more feeling in our hearts.
. . . I live quite tranquil under my curtains, waiting with patience, thanks to Caro's care, to books and dreams, the healing which the sun will bring me. I like this almost complete retreat from the rest of the world; for I am not such an enemy to solitude as you may fancy; and there are in me quite strong tastes and needs which the warmest lovers of a country life would not disavow. I hope that God will cause these thoughts to be matured and, at the same time, the means of realising them.

"M. Buquet came to see me the day of your departure, a few hours after. He came again yesterday to *talk* with me, as you wished. He is to pay another visit next week; at length I hope all will go on for the best." . . .

An entry in the journal (May 19) of Mdlle. De Guérin affords us another pleasant glimpse of Louise: "A letter from Louise, full of interest for you, nothing but heart, spirit, charm from one end to the other; a way of speaking that they only have amongst those heights of Rayssac. The solitude causes this. Ideas come there, the like of which there are nowhere else in the world—unknown, beautiful as flowers or mosses. Charming Louise, how I love her! I find her this time in a calm, a *désabusé*, which astonishes me; she generally has some illusion. I am going to join the other Louise, who so much resembles this one (do you not find it so?), and who prays for your recovery. 'The other day,' she writes to me (Louise de Rayssac), 'I was at the Platér parish church with my aunt; I approached a saintly girl who frequents this church from morning to evening, and who is greatly respected for her piety. I raised a corner of her black veil, and said to her very low: "Pardon, Mdlle., I wish to ask for prayers for a sick young man, brother of the person whom I love the most in the world." "Well, I will pray," she said to me, with that air of modesty which raised her still more in my esteem. I have not seen her again.' Is not this a pretty, pious trait, my brother, this young lady seeking prayers for you with an air of celestial interest? She is charming."

April 24, her journal contains this entry: "How all is laughing, what life the sun has, how sweet and light is the air! A letter, news of the best, dear invalid, and all is changed for me—within, without. *I am happy to-day.*"

Maurice, however, grew so alarmingly worse that it soon became apparent that if he were to see his own old home again no time was to be lost. Probably a presentiment of his approaching end made Maurice desire to die at Le Cayla. During her travels Eugénie received information that he had set out thither with his wife, and he wished her to join them at Tours. Hastening thither, they proceeded by easy steps to Le Cayla, arriving there on July 8, 1839.

As these two lives were so closely united, the rest of that of the brother may be fittingly quoted from the sister's journal, written some time after the bitterness of the last parting.

"It was on July 8, twenty days from our leaving Paris, at nearly six o'clock in the evening, that we came in sight of Le Cayla, the land of hope, the resting-place of our poor invalid. His thoughts had been there only, as the one place on earth, for a long time. I never saw in him a more ardent desire, and it grew more and more keen as we approached. One might have said that he was in a hurry to arrive, to be in time to die there. Had he any presentiment of his end? In the first transports of joy at the sight of Le Cayla, he pressed the hand of Erembert, who was by his side. He made a sign to us all as of a discovery, to me who had never less emotion of pleasure. I was contemplating sorrowfully everything in this sad return, even my sister, and my father, who were at some little distance, coming to meet us. Distressing meeting! My father was dismayed; Marie wept at seeing Maurice. He was so changed, so wasted, so pale, so shaky upon his horse, that he hardly seemed alive. It was terrifying. The journey had killed him. If the thought of arriving had not sustained him, I doubt whether he would have accomplished it. You know something of what he had to suffer, poor dear martyr! He embraced his father and his sister without showing himself to be much moved. At the first sight of the chateau he seemed in a sort of ecstasy; the perturbation that it caused him was unique, and must have exhausted all his faculty of sensation; I never saw him so keenly touched by anything again. He, however, affectionately greeted the reapers who were cutting our wheat, shook hands with some of them, and with all the servants who gathered round us.

"When we came to the salon : 'Ah, how nice it is here,' said he, sitting down on the couch, and he again embraced my father. We were all regarding him with content. It was still a family joy. His wife went to do some unpacking; I took her place beside him, and kissing him on the brow, which I had not done for a long time, said, 'How well you look! You will quickly recover here.' '*I hope so*—I am at home.' 'Let your wife also consider herself as at home; make her understand that she is one of the family, and do as in her own house.' 'No doubt, no doubt.' I do not remember what other things we said in those moments while we were alone. Caroline came down, supper was announced, which Maurice found delicious.

He ate of everything with appetite. 'Ah!' he said to Marie, 'your cooking is excellent.'

"My God! what followed takes hold of my heart. My life is there only.

"I have a future only by faith, by bonds which are attached to Maurice, and from him to the skies. . . .

"But let us return to his life—to the last and precious recollections of it which are left to me.

"We hoped much from the climate, from his native air, and from the warm temperature of our South. The second day from our arrival it was cold; the invalid felt it, and had shiverings. His finger-ends were like ice. I saw clearly that there was not the improvement we had hoped, that he could not recover so quickly whilst these attacks returned. There was no fever after, and the doctor reassured us. These doctors are often deceived, or deceivers. We induced the invalid not to leave his room the following day, attributing the chill he had taken to the coldness of the salon. He resigned himself, as he always did, though somewhat unwillingly, to what we wished; but it was so dull up there, and it became so warm by-and-bye, that I myself invited him to come down.

'Oh! yes,' he said, 'Here I am far from everybody. There is more life below with you all, and then there is the terrace. I will go there to take a walk. Let us go down.' That terrace especially drew him to enjoy the outside air, the sun, and that beautiful nature which he so much loved. I believe it was on that day that he pulled some weeds round the pomegranate tree, and dug some feet of Peruvian lilies. Assisted by his wife he stretched a wire along the wall for the jasmine and creepers. That appeared to amuse him. "So each day I will try my strength a little," said he, on returning indoors. He never went out again. The weakness increased, the least movement fatigued him. He only left his armchair by necessity, or to take a few steps, at the prayer of his wife, who tried everything to draw him from his lethargy. She sang, she played, and all often without effect—at least, I was not able to see any impression. He remained the same to everything, his head leaning upon the side of his chair, his eyes closed. He had, however, some better times some brief periods in which there were flashes towards life. It was in one of these moments that he went to the piano and played an air—poor air, which I shall have in my heart always.

"I wish to tell you, also, how much this dear brother has given me consolation in regard to his Christian sentiments. This dates, not from his last days only; he had kept Easter at Paris. At the beginning of Lent he wrote to me: 'The Abbé Buquel came to see me; to-morrow he will come again to talk with me as you desired.' Dear friend! Yes, I had desired that for his happiness, and he had done it for mine, not conceding for complacency, but doing it from *conviction;* he was incapable of the appearance of an act of faith. I have seen him alone at Tours, in his room on Sunday reading prayers. For some time he had enjoyed works of piety, and I have been thankful that I left with him Saint Theresa and Fénélon, which have done him much good. God ceased not to inspire me for him. So I had the fancy to bring for the journey a good little book, pious and charming to read, translated from the Italian—'Father Quadrupani'—which gave him much pleasure. From time to time he asked me to read him a few pages: 'Read me a little of Quadrupani.' He listened with attention, then signed to me when he had had enough, reflected thereon, closed his eyes and rested, impressing upon his mind the sweet and comforting holy thoughts. Thus every day at Cayla we read to him some sermons of Bossuet and some passages from 'The Imitation of Christ.' He also wished to have some entertaining reading, and having nothing new in our library, we began Scott's 'Old Mortality.' He went through one volume with some appearance of interest, and then gave it up. He was soon fatigued with anything; we did not know what to do in order to divert him. Visits brought him little relief; he talked only with his doctor—a man of intelligence, who pleased the invalid and sustained his interest. I noticed these moral influences, and even in his greatest prostration that intelligent nature rose up with every kindred touch. Thus the evening, or evening but one, before his death he laughed heartily at your *feuilleton*, so pleasantly witty: *Il faut que jeunesse se passe*, with which he was charmed. He wished to have it read over again: 'Write to d'Aurevilly,' he said to me, 'and tell him it is a long time since I have laughed as I have just done.' Alas! he laughed no more! You gave him the last intellectual pleasure that he had. Everything was enjoyable that came to him from you. Friendship was the sweetest and strongest of his sentiments, that which he felt the most deeply, of which he loved best to speak, and which, I can say, he has taken with him to the tomb. *Oh! yes, he loved you to the end.* I do not know on what occasion, being alone with him, speaking of you, I said to him : 'Do you like me to write to your friend?' '*Do I like it?*' he said, with his heart in his voice. The same day, on leaving him, I sent you a bulletin.

"We thought him very weak; however, I hoped always. I had written to the Prince of Hohenlohe. I expected a miracle. His cough was easier, his appetite sustained him. The fatal evening he yet dined with us : the last family dinner! There were some figs which he wished for, and which I was unkind enough to forbid; but the others having approved, he ate one, which did him neither good nor harm, and I was saved from the bitterness of having deprived him of something. ·I wish to tell everything, to preserve every incident of his last moments, much grieved not to remember more. A word that he said to my father has stayed with me. My poor father returned from Gaillac quite hot, with his medicines. When Maurice saw him he said, holding out his hand to him, 'One must confess that you love your children well.' And, indeed, my father did love him well! A little time after the poor invalid, rising with difficulty from his chair to go into the adjoining room, 'I am very low,' he said, speaking as to himself. I heard him, that sentence of death from his mouth, without answering a word, without, perhaps, quite believing it. But I was struck. In the evening they carried him with his chair into his room. While he was going to bed I talked with Erembert: 'He is very feeble to-night, but his chest is freer, the cough is gone. If we can get on to the month of October he will be saved.' It was the 18th July, at ten o'clock at night. He had a bad night. I heard his wife speak to him, rising often. All was heard in my room—I listened to all. I went soon in the morning to see him, and his look struck me. It was a fixed look. 'What does it mean?' I said to the doctor, who came early. 'It means that Maurice is worse.' Ah, my God!. Erembert went to tell my father, who came quickly. He went immediately out, and consulted with the doctor, who had told him it was necessary to think of the last sacraments. The Curé was sent for, also my sister, who was at church. My father begged the doctor, M. Facien, to prepare Caroline for the terrible tidings. He took her apart. I went to join her immediately, and found her all in tears. I heard her say, 'I knew it.' She knew that he must die! 'For three months I have been preparing myself for this sacrifice.' Thus the stroke of death did not terrify her, but she was disconsolate.

"'My poor sister,' I said, putting my arm round her neck. 'This is the dreadful moment; but let us not weep; we must tell him, he must be prepared for the sacraments. Do you feel strong enough for the duty, or shall I do it?' 'Yes; you do it, Eugénie— you do it!' She was stifled with sobs. I passed immediately to the bed of the invalid, and, praying God to sustain me, I leant over him, and kissed him on the moist forehead. 'My brother,' I said to him, 'I want to tell you something. I have written for you to the Prince of Hohenlohe. You know he has done some miracles of healing. God works by whom He wills and how He wills. He is, above all, the sovereign healer of the sick. Have you not confidence in him? Supreme confidence' (or *full*, I do not remember which). 'Well, my friend, let us ask in all confidence His mercy; let us unite in prayers, we with the Church, you in your heart. We are going to have Mass with Communion. You will have it with us. Jesus Christ went to the sick, you know.' 'Oh! I wish it much, I wish to unite in your prayers.' 'That is right, my brother; the Curé is coming, and you will confess. It will not pain you to talk to the Curé?' 'Not at all.' The Curé came. Maurice asked him to wait a little, not being quite ready. We saw him entirely collected and meditative. Alas! last meditation of his soul! In about ten minutes he called for the priest, and remained with him for nearly half-an-hour, conversing, we were told, with all the lucidity and calmness of mind he had when in health. We made the arrangements necessary for the Communion. His wife, with the sadness and piety of an angel, recited to him the prayers for the Communion, which are so beautiful, and those for the dying, which are so touching; then he asked for those for the extreme unction, calmly and naturally, as for a thing expected.

"He was hungry and faint, and asked me for his cordial, which I brought him. As he perspired much, I said to him, 'My dear, do not put out your arm; I will feed you like an infant.' A smile came upon his lips, where I laid the spoon, where I made to pass the last food he took. Thus I have been able to serve him once more, to give him my care another time. He was given back to me dying. I marked it as a favour of God, granted to my love as a sister, that I have rendered to this dear brother the last services to the soul and body, since I prepared him for the last sacraments, and made his last nourishment: food for both lives. This seems nothing, is nothing, in fact, for any one else. It is for me alone to observe it, and to thank Providence for these relations taken up again with my dear Maurice before he left us. Sad and indefinable compensation for so many months of passive friendship! Was I wrong in wishing to serve him? Who knows? . . .

"The invalid, it seemed to me, was better. His eyes, open again, had not the startling fixed appearance of the morning, nor was his intellect feeble; he appeared morally revived, and in full enjoyment of his faculties throughout the ceremonies. He followed everything with his heart, very devoutly. . . . He pressed the hand of the Curé, who continued to speak to him of heaven, put to his lips a cross that his wife offered him, and then began to sink. We all kissed him, and he died, Friday morning, July 19, 1839, at half-past eleven. It was eleven days after our arrival at Le Cayla—eight months after his marriage."

With the life of her brother the brightness of that of Eugénie passed away. Though they had been destined to be so much separated, she had lived for him. After he was gone she was possessed by thoughts of him, and a desire to do justice to his memory and genius became the dominating power of her life. Returning from his graveside, she sits down to open a fresh page in her journal, heading it: " Still to him—to Maurice dead, to Maurice in heaven. He was the glory and the joy of my heart. Oh, it is a sweet name and full of dilection, the name of brother." On this, his burial day, she writes : " No, my brother, death shall not separate us, nor take thee from my thought: death separates only the body; the soul instead of being there is in heaven, but this change of abode takes away nothing of its affections. They are far from that, I hope; they love better in heaven, where all is glorified. Oh, my dear Maurice, Maurice! Art thou far from me? Dost thou hear me?"

In the midst of her profound grief it was a source of great consolation to Eugénie that her brother had returned to the faith and love of his early days. Her letters to her friends are henceforth full of Maurice. Memories of him throng her thought, and find outlet only in outpourings of tender love; reflections on the sadness, the partings of life, the hopes of reunion in the life to come, which alone sustained her; prayers for the peace of the departed soul. Her life for the future was to be more intensely spiritual. One earthly care only was left—her brother's memory. She continued her journal for some months, still writing to Maurice as if for his eye. This may seem to be unnatural, arising from an over-sensitive and morbid state of mind. She, indeed, came to this conclusion herself; and, after a time, addressed her journal no longer to her brother, but to his latest friend at Paris.

The genius of Maurice de Guérin, so slowly recognised during his life, began to be acknowledged after his death. Madame Georges Sand wrote an appreciative review in an essay upon his life, poems, and letters in the *Revue des Deux Mondes* of May, 1840. Other articles followed. His contributions, journal, letters, and fragments were collected, as far as possible, with the idea of publishing a book of his literary remains. Eugénie herself made a journey to Paris for the purpose of furthering the design. She rejoiced in the idea of justice being done to her brother's memory, and the true side of his character presented to the world. Her hopes were, however, doomed to disappointment. The latest entry in her journal is made the last day of the year 1840, and is :. "My God, how sad is time, whether it be that which goes or that which comes! And how right the saint was when he said, Let us throw our hearts in eternity."

Difficulties in the way of the publication of her brother's writings arose from one cause or another, and, after a long sojourn in Paris and Nevers, she was obliged to return home to Le Cayla with the remaining ambition of her life unfulfilled. A large collection of papers, which had been placed in the hands of her brother's friend, were neglected, and difficulty was experienced in getting them returned. When eventually, through the intervention of a friend, they were restored, the design had been abandoned.

Time, meanwhile, brought its inevitable changes in the quiet home of Le Cayla. Her friend Louise de Bayne left her home among the mountains to be married to a husband whom she accompanied to Algiers, Caroline returned to India; her brother Erembert married, and baby feet came again to resound within the old walls. But Eugénie's heart was in the tomb with her dead brother and her buried hopes. Her health declined. She died at Le Cayla on May 31, 1848. A short time before she died, it is said that she gave the key of a certain drawer to her sister, requesting her to burn the papers she would find there, and adding, "All is but vanity."

What the devoted sister failed to see accomplished during her life has, happily, been done since. The surviving sister, with the help of friends, set herself to the task not only of rescuing from oblivion the writings of Maurice, but also those of the gifted Eugénie herself. The "Journal, Letters, and Poems" of Maurice, published in 1860, has passed through many editions. This was followed by the journal of Eugénie, and afterwards by her letters, both of which have had a still greater popularity than the works of Maurice. These books contain truly the record of a soul's life. Their character is to some extent shown by the extracts contained herein; but their real value is only to be seen, and their charm enjoyed, by a loving perusal. Her letters have a grace entirely their own. Her journal reveals a depth of thought, a wonderful insight into and appreciation of truth and beauty, a store of devotional reflection, which render it a work of rare worth. Literary fame was far from her thoughts. If she wrote at all it must be gracefully. She says: "I often ask myself, of what profit is all this writing, but that it pleases Maurice, who finds his sister there. Still, if it affords me innocent amusement; pauses of rest in the day's work. If I garner these my flowers, gathered in solitude, my thoughts, my reflections, that God sends me for instruction and comfort, there is no harm in it. And if some one finds here and there a true thought, and feels it, and is better for it, though only for a moment, I shall have done good—the good I want to do."

It is, however, in Eugénie's memory as a sister that this record of her is here given. And she stands out for all time as an example of one of the world's most devoted sisters. Her depth of love, her intense sympathy, her self-sacrificing zeal, her unswerving purpose, her deep piety, were all directed or intensified by the master passion of her soul—

the love of her brother—and we cannot but believe that such love brings its reward, that is not only for time, but that, immortal as its origin, it has, at last, been fully satisfied.

BY THE SAME AUTHOR.

DOROTHY WORDSWORTH:

The Story of a Sister's Love.

LONDON: JAMES CLARKE & CO.   Price 3s. 6d.

SOME OPINIONS OF THE PRESS.

THE LITERARY WORLD.—This "STORY OF A SISTER'S LOVE" will, we should imagine, be read with delighted satisfaction by all who have come to feel an interest in Wordsworth and his home and family. It is a most welcome and interesting book. We give it a very hearty commendation, and are sure it will have a loving welcome from Wordsworthians of all sorts and conditions.

THE CHRISTIAN WORLD.—Told with considerable skill and feeling. We have found it to be a very fascinating story, and have unfeigned pleasure in commending it to our readers. The story of that life of devotion has left a tender and powerful lesson for many.

GREENWICH OBSERVER.—This is a delightful book, and one that will be much appreciated by Wordsworthian students. The story is told with considerable detail, and in a manner calculated to rouse very tender emotions in all who read it. Admirers of Wordsworth will be exceedingly thankful to Mr. Lee for filling this vacancy in the list of notable Englishwomen. It is the story of a life rich in that blended strength and grace of character which made Dorothy Wordsworth loved by women and reverenced by men. We commend the book, to earnest and thoughtful young women especially, as a volume that is intensely interesting and full of noble impulse.

WAKEFIELD FREE PRESS.—All admirers of the poet Wordsworth will be pleased to learn that an admirably-written biography of the poet's sister Dorothy, by Edmund Lee, has just been issued. Mr. Lee's choice and arrangement of his material is admirable.

WEST CUMBERLAND TIMES.—Every member of the Wordsworth Association should become acquainted with the new work from the pen of Edmund Lee, of Bradford. Every tourist halting beneath the hoary yews of Grasmere Churchyard, and honouring the graves of the Wordsworth household, should first be versed in the biography of Dorothy Wordsworth and her sweet example of sisterly love. We heartily commend the book.

CONTEMPORARY REVIEW.—To Lake literature " Dorothy Wordsworth " is a pleasant addition.

AMBLESIDE HERALD.—We can remember no life of the poet which so vividly brings to light the immense influence which the sister exercised over her brother. Addressing those (if any) who are still unacquainted with the life of the Rydal bard, we would say:

> If in thine inmost soul there chance to dwell
> Aught of the poetry of human life,
> Take thou this book, and with a humble heart
> Follow these pilgrims in their joyous walk,

ILLUSTRATED LONDON NEWS.—An appreciative monograph, presenting a pleasing picture of this remarkable woman.

MANCHESTER EXAMINER AND TIMES.—In performing what has evidently been a labour of love he has produced a singularly charming biography. The book is one to which we extend a hearty welcome. The writer modestly speaks of it as a compilation, and such, indeed, it largely is; but there are compilations and compilations, and the present volume is more artistically harmonious and homogeneous in construction than many works of more obtrusive originality. Mr. Edmund Lee's name is new to us, but we shall be glad to hear of him again.

THE BOSTON LITERARY WORLD.—An agreeable and valuable narrative. He has done his work with sympathy and good taste.

THE CHURCH, (PHIL.)—A charming memoir, and will supply its readers with pleasure, instruction and moral power.

THE NATION.—The whole volume breathes the peace, quiet pleasures, and domesticity of Wordsworth's home; the closing chapters, which contain in a few words the story of how his sister's mind became weakened and dull in consequence of a severe illness, and how the care of her was one of the poet's most cherished occupations in his last aged years, are full of pathos.

UTICA PRESS.—Mr. Lee pays a beautiful tribute to the memory of Dorothy Wordsworth. It is a charming book, exceedingly graceful in style, abounding in interest from the first page to the last—in fact, it is one of the most delightful biographies written for many a day.

DAYTON DEMOCRAT.—The author modestly claims for himself no more credit than is due to a compiler; a claim, how-

OPINIONS OF THE PRESS.

ever, which those who read his book will be disposed to dispute. . . . It is a mosaic so nicely fitted together, and pervaded by the appreciative spirit of her biographer that it seizes upon the reader with the inexpressible charm of a well-written book.

BOSTON COURIER.—Mr. Lee has written enthusiastically, yet with judicious restraint. The tender regard of the brother and sister, their close intellectual union, and the influence Dorothy had upon the development of the poet's genius, are clearly shown and well treated. The book adds to the reader's knowledge of Wordsworth, by presenting his character in a new point of view, and will be heartily welcomed by all lovers of the poet.

PITTSBURGH CHRISTIAN ADVOCATE.—The author has rendered valuable service. With fidelity, delicacy and true appreciation of her character and worth, he presents the life of this excellent woman.

NEW YORK INDEPENDENT.—A delightful sketch. An altogether charming book.

NEW YORK TIMES.—It may be said, as praise of Mr. Lee's monograph, that he prepares the reader to accept without criticism his final declaration that Dorothy Wordsworth was the most perfect sister the world hath seen.

BOSTON GAZETTE.—Told with a literary skill that makes it very interesting reading.

BOSTON TRAVELLER.—He writes with enthusiasm and charm of style.

BOSTON COMMONWEALTH.—An altogether delightful book.

PHILADELPHIA BULLETIN.—The volume has a peculiar charm.

PHILADELPHIA RECORD.—The delightful and simple manner in which he has done his work, and the impress of his individuality, which he has left on almost every page, give the book a decided originality.

PALLADIUM.—Just and appreciative. Will fill a long-felt want.

CHICAGO JOURNAL.—The book has a singular sweetness and charm about it.

THE CRITIC.—An idyll surely, and one which could scarcely be better told than in the volume before us. The writing of the book has evidently been a labour of love with Mr. Lee, and it has been even better done than such labours are apt to be. It is a delightful picture that he gives us of William and Dorothy.

www.ingramcontent.com/pod-product-compliance
Lightning Source LLC
Chambersburg PA
CBHW030320240426
43673CB00040B/1222